THE SOHO GUIDE

Also by Joanna Bawa

THE COMPUTER USER'S HEALTH HANDBOOK

THE SOHO GUIDE

Earning Money with Home Computing

JOANNA BAWA AND MANEK DUBASH

SOUVENIR PRESS

First published 1996 by
Souvenir Press Ltd,
43 Great Russell Street, London WC1B 3PA
and simultaneously in Canada

ISBN 0 285 63284 1

Typeset by Galleon Typesetting, Ipswich
Printed in Great Britain by
The Guernsey Press Company Ltd, Guernsey, Channel Islands

Contents

Acknowledgements

The help, advice, patience and expertise of the following are gratefully acknowledged:

Vyla Rollins of KPMG; Andrew Bibby, Chris Lewis, Karan Bawa—and everyone on CompuServe whose contributions to the libraries and discussion groups proved such a rich vein of information. In particular, thanks to the sysops and members of the Working from Home Forum, Telework Europa Forum, Entrepreneurs' Forum, PR and Marketing Forum, UK Professionals Forum and Executives On-Line.

J.B.
M.D.

1 Working From Home: The Opportunities

So you bought a computer. Perhaps it was for yourself, perhaps for your children, but what are you really getting out of it? For many of us computers undoubtedly represent the forefront of today's technology. Computing and technology-related words are appearing with increasing frequency in the newspapers, on radio and television and in the conversations going on around us, and this can be as good a reason to buy one as any other. But they are not cheap, and it is a common enough experience to unwrap the new machine, look up a couple of entries in the CD-ROM based encyclopaedia, write a letter to your grandmother—and then leave it to gather dust. Of course, your children may adopt it as a games station, but even so you may well end up wondering why you shelled out upwards of two thousand pounds for a machine that does little more than a typewriter or a pocket calculator.

In fact computers do much more than typewriters or calculators. Most of us know that and have probably begun to experience their capabilities for ourselves in the workplace, but have not yet thought about their possibilities in the home. Maybe you carry a portable machine around sometimes or use a modem to dial into distant computers, but still feel that you are not getting enough out of your rapidly depreciating investment.

This book is about getting more out of your home computer. It is written with a particular aim in mind—to enable people with any combination of enthusiasm, time and technology on their hands to combine these elements more productively. This does not necessarily mean making money, but usually that will be an objective, so we have included sections on the legal and taxation issues associated with this. We have also addressed parts of the book to another large and growing group: people who are in full-time employment and would like to use technology to achieve a more flexible working life (and a correspondingly more fulfilling personal life). If any of this describes you or your objectives, it is possible you could be getting a lot more out of the technology available.

COMPUTERS AT HOME—WHO CAN BENEFIT?

Used to its full capacity, today's technology can be immensely liberating. There are several groups of people who stand to gain when they learn more about computer power:

Established and aspiring small offices and home offices

A rapidly growing use of computers outside the corporation is within the SOHO market (small office home office), a term which describes professional or profit-making activities within the home or a private office, typically using computer power as a key element. In common usage, 'small' and 'home' office mean pretty much the same thing—in this book, 'small office' should be taken to mean a set-up where the main aim is profit, whereas 'home office' refers to an arrangement whereby you are employed by an external organisation and occasionally (or regularly) working at home, perhaps to keep up with office work or to handle those extra assignments which might mean a later promotion.

SO—small offices
Even if you are planning to stay small, it is essential for small businesses to develop and maintain a competitive edge with computer power. Broadly speaking, there are two main types of 'small office' which require computing power to stay alive:

- *Self-employed entrepreneurs* working for their own profit, on a full-time basis.
- *Part-time entrepreneurs*, who have another job but 'moonlight' from their home offices.

The SO market is usually defined to include small offices with fewer than ten employees and home-based businesses. It is growing rapidly, and in the USA these small offices are expected to spend over US$14 billion in product sales by 1996. Much of the appeal of this type of business is fuelled by recent technological advances in personal computers, software, modems, faxes and other items, which have made it possible for entrepreneurs to reap large rewards for a relatively small outlay.

HO—home offices

The home office is occupied by growing bands of aspiring and established *telecommuters*. Aspirants to this lifestyle take their work home at night or at weekends and use a home office to get the job done, whilst their more established colleagues may spend whole chunks of their working week at home on a regular basis. In terms of numbers, it is the telecommuting community that is growing the fastest, perhaps because the benefits to all are easier to see. In large cities, for example, employees often spend 12 hours a week just commuting to and from their office buildings; companies are starting to see that employees can use those hours more productively by working at a home office.

Telecommuting is becoming increasingly popular in the UK among larger companies, typically with more than 1,000 employees, or those that are located in heavily congested areas such as London and the South-East. Among the benefits associated with telecommuting are higher worker productivity, lower staff turnover, the ability to employ more disabled workers and environmental benefits, all of which are powerful arguments for continuing this practice. The disadvantages cited by opponents are the need to evolve and adapt to a new style of management; and the social isolation inherent in work-at-home situations. On the whole, however, the pros far outweigh the cons—forward-looking organisations and their employees are increasingly moving towards part-time telecommuting, in which staff members work at home one or two days a week and in the office for the remainder of the week.

The SOHO market covers most aspects of non-corporate business or professional computing, but within these broad terms there are groups who stand to gain particular benefits from home-based computer power. These benefits need not be profit-orientated, but it is surprising how easy it can be to turn them towards such an aim. Apart from anything else, computing at home opens up a huge range of possibilities for people who would otherwise be excluded from any kind of business or technology-related activity.

Older people

Until now it has been difficult for older workers to find new, challenging employment in the face of youthful competition. Home-based computing can—and is beginning to—change all that if one is prepared to acquire basic computing skills. It is not simply a question of availability, either; older workers who are willing to tackle the technology are proving to be more available, more reliable and more committed than many younger people. And without the need for career visibility and progression of their upstart peers, older people are far more likely to adapt well to the 'downside' of isolated telecommuting. Managers who are still resistant to telecommuting are often more open to older employees, because they are perceived as having longer work histories and fewer distractions at home, particularly children; older workers are also often better suited to part-time or shared jobs. At the very least, telecommuting for older employees can serve as a phased retirement tool, allowing the worker to taper off from the job and at the same time get used to spending more time at home. And for the potential small business person, age is no more a barrier than gender: computers don't care who is tapping the keyboard.

Women at home and in business

The career/family dilemma has always been a peculiarly female one, and too many women still find that there is simply no satisfactory solution. Child care often precludes serious commitment to a career and the best most women can hope for is a compromise: costly child-minders, no further promotion and a lot of guilt. Planned and used carefully, however, computers can provide a means to help escape this trap. The home office can provide a flexible solution for women who cannot always get into the office when their children are young, and it need not detract from their professional productivity—in fact, by removing the stresses of physical commuting, telecommuting can greatly enhance women's output. A number of studies confirm what most people know intuitively: women are, on the whole, less concerned than men with career success at all costs, but instead seek a balance between career ambitions and family and personal needs. Telecommuting is instantly more appealing to women, since it offers a more direct route to this balance.

It is also the case that computer power has become the most effective route by which women can get into business, and female entrepreneurs are flourishing, enjoying the autonomy and control that computers confer. Across the board, more women than ever before are setting up on their own, perhaps encouraged by an uncertain economic climate and a general move towards more part-time and short-term jobs. Whilst many of these may not begin by establishing a small office, it is more than likely that the greater proportion will come to rely on some combination of computer-driven technology in order to stay up and running.

In between these two groups of women is a third group— women who are at home without full-time employment, either because of children or economic circumstances, but who are not really interested in the full business adventure. The beauty of home-based computer power is that it need not become a full-scale business: there are many niches into which home-based users can fit without becoming committed entrepreneurs.

People with disabilities

Dispassionate and objective treatment is something many disabled people long for in what is undoubtedly a harsh and competitive environment, and whilst its robotic behaviour may be the computer's least attractive attribute, it is also its most valuable. 'Brain' skills are no more the prerogative of the able-bodied than are emotions, and computers provide the means by which the intellectual capabilities of disabled people can shine through.

Redundant executives and the unemployed

The gloom of redundancy and unemployment cannot be cured by a computer, but it can be offset. At the very least, ownership of a home computer (or borrowership of someone else's) can help keep your keyboard and software skills up to date, which in turn can maintain confidence and opportunities; because computers are still widely perceived as difficult and frightening, people with basic computing skills and the confidence to learn more are still a highly sought-after commodity. For the more adventurous, a computer and modem can provide an exhaustive job-search tool, trawling the many (and increasing) email and bulletin board systems available, whilst simultaneously providing high visibility to potential employers. And if you are feeling really brave, computer power can help turn your years of accumulated experience into marketable skills and do the marketing for you.

THE DOWNSIDE: PRACTICAL AND PSYCHOLOGICAL CONSIDERATIONS

The enormous potential of working at home should not blind you to the snags, nor should it be assumed that telecommuting will inevitably improve everyone's life. Before committing yourself to a home-based working life, you need to consider how well it will suit your temperament and psychological needs, as well as practical issues such as household maintenance and child care. It is too easy to assume, for example, that a home-based worker can readily accommodate children's school hours and entertainment needs, do the shopping, wash the dishes and make the beds as part of her daily routine. Not only is this impractical and unfair, it can also severely undermine the home-worker's self-esteem and belief in the importance of her work. These issues are dealt with in more depth in later chapters.

WHAT'S GOING ON OUT THERE, AND WHY SHOULD I BE INTERESTED?

Potential telecommuters clearly have a lot to gain from a home office. Even if money is not involved, at least electronic travellers can reconstruct their lifestyles to make more time for personal and family commitments without compromising their professional activities. And for small office enthusiasts, the opportunities could scarcely be riper. If you are (or want to become) an entrepreneur, you will already understand the immense contribution that technology can make.

You may never have thought seriously about setting up your own business—maybe you have actively avoided that route, not wishing to get involved in the administrative, financial and legal headaches. And if you are already employed, it is obviously neither practical nor desirable. But getting more out of your home computer need not mean becoming a serious entrepreneur—the point is, it can already do a lot more for you than you probably realise, and although it will not cost any money to explore your options, you could well end up making some.

For whatever reason and whoever paid for it—if you have a computer sitting there, why not make the most of it?

CONSTRUCTIVE THINGS COMPUTER OWNERS CAN DO

Games may be addictive, but they don't enrich your life (quite the reverse, if you are not careful). Letters are useful, but you can do those with a typewriter (or even a pen and paper), and those mouse-drawn pictures are simply going nowhere.

So what is there for the computer owner to do? Lots of things. Since the emergence of the personal computer (PC) in the early eighties, things have changed beyond all recognition in many of the markets with which you may be familiar. The most important trend is that skills which once had to be acquired slowly and painfully over a number of years and hoarded (to be farmed out at great expense) by specialists, are now readily available to the astute PC owner. You can see this trend in many offices and large corporations: typing pools are disappearing as managers and executives are increasingly required to use word processors to create their own letters and reports; secretarial jobs are diminished as administration and time-scheduling become routine applications of the computer. Even specialist or professional skills—accountancy, graphic design and research, for example—are easily accessible to the honest computer user with a bit of interest and enthusiasm. It cannot continue for ever, of course—there is nothing to be gained by having highly paid executives spend their time performing chores far better suited to administrative and clerical staff, so many tasks which have been computerised can be devolved to others.

Attitude, experience and expectation inhibit many people from taking more advantage of the power available to them. Too many of us still leave large elements of our jobs to other people, believing that they are better at them or more knowledgeable than we are. True, many areas of computing still benefit from a little natural talent—no computer can turn turgid prose into a sparkling novel; nor can it render amateur scribbles into high art—but there are vast areas that remain unknown and unexplored. With relatively little time and experience, it is possible for the naturally talented to channel their skills into much more profitable areas, and for the competent generalists to become hard-nosed experts in at least one specialist area.

There are probably hundreds of jobs that you can perform

from home. The common factor that makes them 'telework-able' is their structure; most importantly, all involve a stage or phase which requires thought and isolation, but not complex equipment or team input. The jobs described below involve three steps: preparation, production, and presentation.

1 *Preparation* usually means interviewing or researching, and gathering necessary materials. The home-worker can do this either by visiting in person, telephoning or dialling in, by modem, to remote electronic libraries and research sources.

2 *Production* means converting information or raw materials and specifications into a product—whether that be a report, a program, a floppy disk of stored data or a marketing proposal. Clearly, this comprises the bulk of the home-worker's 'work', thinking, planning and interacting directly with a computer at home.

3 *Presentation* refers to the hand-over from the worker to his or her client, either physically or via modem.

Home-working is eminently suitable for jobs that are composed of these stages, since theoretically all three can be performed from the desk. In many instances, however, it is likely that preparation and presentation will involve travel and face-to-face contact, which may also be preferable psychologically.

Keyboard and literary

Word processing and data entry
If you can type, you are already ahead of the game. Despite the spread of keyboards and computers, very few people ever undergo any sort of formal keyboard training, but teach themselves an awkward 'hunt-and-peck' style instead. Whilst this may satisfy occasional needs, it is often too painful and time-consuming a style for people who have regular or lengthy writing requirements. Typing may simply be a task they lack the time to take on themselves, or the hated job within a small business which cannot cost-justify a

full-time secretary. Word processing represents an opportunity for the home-based user to take on these responsibilities, especially if you have a good understanding of the
software you are using and can apply its capabilities confidently. Typical needs may be secretarial or administrative,
and data entry.

Feature writing
Writing and journalism are an attractive option for home-
based computer users, often because they seem to represent
autonomy, flexibility and relatively interesting work which
anyone can have a go at. Whilst this is true once you are
established or have the luxury of regular work, the life of the
freelance writer is notoriously erratic and a difficult objective to achieve. It also requires good basic writing skills
and a reasonably sound knowledge of your chosen subject
area. There is a wide range of books which can advise on
how to get started in a particular field, but it is well worth
knowing how technology can give you an extra edge. For
example, computer power can not only increase the speed
with which you produce good quality, well-presented work,
but it becomes far easier to identify and maintain details of
existing and potential contacts, research new articles and
contact experts in a particular area. It is also worth bearing in
mind that experts in difficult or specialised areas are always
going to be in demand, so if you are, or can become, such a
specialist, there is a greater likelihood that your skills in
writing about that area will be in demand. As a home-based
worker with all the technology that implies, you are already
an expert in a growing, fascinating market.

Technical writing
Quite a different skill from feature writing, technical writing
requires accuracy, precision and a terrier-like ability to extract
clear, useful information from the experts. Technical writing often means instruction manuals, specifications and help
documentation, most of which will be dictated or drafted by
experts who may not have the ability to communicate the
complexities of their products. This may be tedious, but it is

important and necessary (and widely read) work, and represents a secure market for those who are in it. It is also a tremendously useful research experience, since a thorough understanding of your subject is a prerequisite. This can be invaluable for subsequent work, such as technical journalism.

CV preparation/Report and thesis writing

These areas require slightly more than simple keyboard skills, but for this reason can be that much more rewarding. The curriculum vitae still represents an important entry point for anyone seeking a new job or even just an interview, and its formulation and presentation are crucial elements. The preparation of other people's CVs requires interviewing skills to determine what a person has to offer an employer, what sort of employers he or she is approaching and why, and how best to match the two components to achieve success. In doing so, you will need fine judgement to determine which qualifications and achievements should be given priority, perhaps varying these according to the employer or job applied for—the flexibility of today's technology makes this easy.

Graduate theses, student projects and scientific reports and papers are also a small but steady market for the computerised home-worker. In some cases these may require familiarity with technical or scientific terms, but more useful will be an understanding of the notation and layout requirements of such reports. References, for example, are always written in a particular style which must be adhered to.

That novel . . .

For the seriously committed only, That Novel must surely represent the aspirations of everyone who ever sat down at a keyboard and realised how easy it *could* be. Writing novels (and getting them published!) is the subject of many existing books and not something to be tackled here, but don't expect your computer to become the motivation, the means or the inspiration for any sort of worthwhile fiction. Instead, if you're serious about That Novel, you can look to your PC to provide you with an easier and more flexible blank page, extensive storage space and a good printing facility. And if your novel requires research, a modem can be the link that achieves this. Otherwise—good luck!

Artistic, design and creative

Illustration/design

Professional illustration and design are not really appropriate as home-based pursuits unless you already have the talent, experience and training. If you do, perhaps from a previous job, they can be lucrative and convenient home-based skills. Those who can combine a genuine drawing or design talent with a good understanding of the software intended for these skills are rare indeed—too many gifted artists shun technology as superfluous to their needs. But electronic images and designs are needed as badly as are words and numbers, and if you can create them to look as good as hand-drawn pictures, you can be certain that your skills will be sought after.

Technical design is another highly skilled area which can work well for the experienced home-based worker. Computer-aided design (CAD) and drafting are important and flourishing fields, and work well for home-based users. For the less technical, charting software represents an emerging field of potential growth: the creation of documents containing semi-automated diagrams, flow charts and floor plans is still tricky for those with limited time, so for the home-worker, this represents an opportunity.

Desktop publishing

The power of technology has been profound for those involved in publishing leaflets, newsletters, local magazines and posters. Desktop publishing is a relatively mature software market and for those with the skills to convert natural creativity into eye-catching designs, there is a ripe market. DTP can be used to produce anything from smart price lists for start-up businesses through to full-scale catalogues, and constitutes regular work for many former paper-based designers.

The software available today makes it easy to design newsletters, build stories and edit images—without professional graphics training.

Technical and computing

Programming

Many companies, large and small, use programmers who telecommute. Sometimes these programmers are employed directly, but more usually they are hired to fulfil a specific contract for a specific period of time and may work for more than one client simultaneously. Programming often calls for the peace and quiet that a home office offers and does not impose time restrictions (programmers are notoriously erratic in their working hours, and often nocturnal). When programmers need to tap into their companies' computers, there is no reason why they cannot do so remotely. The ability to access these resources at night, when demand is low, also adds the benefit of quick response time.

Systems analysis

The job of the systems analyst is to convert paper and physical information flows into computer systems. The work begins with site visits and interviews with employees; from there the systems analyst designs the system using mathematical models and cost accounting, a lengthy process that is easily performed at home. Deadlines that call for evening and weekend work, and the likelihood that systems analysts already have the equipment they need to work from home, also make this a good job for teleworkers.

Legal and professional

Stockbroking

Stockbrokers no longer have to work from brokerage houses to monitor stocks. The fabled 'big bang' of the Eighties computerised most of the dealing process and now online services bring the stock market into a stockbroker's home. And since brokerage firms are generally located in big cities where commuting can be difficult, teleworking is especially attractive to stockbrokers.

Accountancy

Many accountants with private rather than corporate clients have worked at home for years, dealing with their clients over the telephone and performing paperwork according to their own hours at home. With its high element of procedure and calculation, accountancy has been a natural convert to the computer and many good software packages now exist to support accounts professionals. When software power is combined with a modem, it becomes much easier to transfer data between client and accountant.

Investment and portfolio management

One of the quickest and most appealing ways to make money has always been to 'buy low, sell high'. For those with the experience and expertise the stock market has always been a source of rich pickings, and now it is easier than ever thanks to computer power. Using a home-based computer and modem, it is possible to dial directly into large databases of share and investment information to get highly accurate and up-to-date information with which to make investment decisions. The database information is updated regularly from all round the world, enabling you to dial in at any time of the day or night, depending on whether you are interested in London, New York or Tokyo prices. Beware, however: better information can only *help* you make your own decisions, it is not an easy way to endless riches!

Network and investigative

Market or scientific research

The availability of immense libraries of information and access to the experts themselves, via the Internet and other electronic networks, has made professional research a viable option for the home-worker. With a modem and PC it is now possible to locate and retrieve information on almost any subject imaginable, which will invariably be in-depth, thorough and recent. Email makes it possible to enter discussions with the authors of such information directly, to identify, for example, new trends or areas justifying particular attention. Once the research information you need is acquired, you can use powerful word processing software to compile concise reports or summaries.

Commercial

Selling

Sales reps have a long history of working from home. Now, with personal computers, modems and fax machines so widely available, there is less incentive than ever for a sales rep to make the trip to company headquarters. Because a sales rep's output is easily measured, managers don't have to worry about managing from afar—a drop in productivity is quickly apparent.

Public relations

Public relations professionals spend a lot of time gathering information and turning it into press releases, technical articles and briefing materials. Established PR professionals who have built up a reputation and client base may find home-working and telecommuting particularly fruitful; in fact, when trying to sell your expertise in technical areas to new clients, positive evidence of your ability to understand and use technology will be an advantage.

Other

Translating

For linguists, translation work maps naturally onto a home office. Apart from the linguistic skills, translation requires peace, quiet and speed, so many translators work by computer and modem, since there is no faster way to transmit information to a client. Some companies, such as Berlitz, actually insist that their translators have computer set-ups.

Proof reading

The checking and correction of written work is another skill easily adapted to the home office. Like translation work, clients can send the raw material over by modem which can be proofed on screen, then re-transmitted back. Bear in mind that proof reading is a lot more complex than simply looking for spelling mistakes, however, so you can also use a computer to build up a list of styles, specialist terms and notations.

2 Making Friends With the Machine: Your Essential Guide

How things have changed over the last ten years! Not so long ago, a computer conjured up for most people visions of a large, air-conditioned room populated by massive, humming boxes. On their fascias, these mainframe computers sported row upon row of flashing lights and were attended by silent, white-coated men, acolytes to the machines. Such machines, somewhat like those deployed by James Bond's deadly foes, do of course still exist, particularly in large or publicly funded organisations. Many big companies still use them to run their businesses, with programs that have been specially developed for the organisation's particular needs, and they are unlikely to throw them away in a hurry, largely because the cost of shifting the programs and information that they contain, often in a specialised format, would be prohibitive.

On the other hand, the growth of the PC, the computer that almost everyone can afford, has been spectacular, and has turned many businesses upside down—almost literally. Many tasks for which you might otherwise have used a specialist, such as a typist, secretary or programmer, can now be done yourself—jobs such as writing and laying out a simple report using word processing and desktop publishing software, or generating a database that meets your needs. It is difficult to think of an application for the PC that is not already catered for by at least one piece, or more likely dozens of pieces, of application software. If you need to send a message to any point on the globe, put together a business presentation, lay out a newsletter, design your kitchen, fly through a graphical representation of your new home or office, or crunch some serious numbers in pursuit of statistical needles in a numeric haystack for a research project, the PC can do it.

Whether or not you already own a computer, if you are reading this book you have obviously decided you want to make more use of the technology available. You may fit into the professional niches described earlier, or you may be an entrepreneur with a great idea and hard-won business skills. You may have lost your office job but not the drive and talent that won it for you in the first place; or you may just want more out of your investment than a games station.

WHAT DO I WANT IN MY HOME OFFICE?

Trends suggest that most home-workers have more, rather than less, powerful machines at home than they do at work. The implication is that home-workers are aware that technology moves on apace and also that they cannot keep on upgrading indefinitely. Each purchase must therefore be the most advanced of its kind available at the time, to delay the moment when they need to buy a better one. On the whole this is good advice—no matter what you already have in terms of equipment, all the subsequent items you buy should be the best and most powerful you can afford.

The computer

The obvious solution here appears to be the *notebook computer*. It is small, portable and neat—what more could you want in your home office? The answer is a full-size *desktop machine*. Do not be taken in by the charms of the notebook: undeniably powerful and attractive though it is, it has a number of shortcomings which will not be apparent immediately. Notebooks have fixed keyboards and tiny screens, both of which are direct and powerful contributors to headache, eyestrain and repetitive strain injury. You cannot sit properly whilst typing and watching the screen, but tend to hunch over your little notebook so that your back goes as well, and there is as yet no satisfactory notebook alternative to the mouse. Two or three hours of continuous use will be all that you can reasonably expect if you have a notebook. Notebooks are irreplaceable when it comes to travelling, however, and if this makes up a large component of your work, you will need to have one. If you need to travel and you cannot afford both a notebook *and* a desktop, you will have to keep a careful eye on the hours you work.

Because the computer is often the biggest piece of equipment in the home office, one space-saving strategy is to find a desktop computer with a small footprint. Another approach is to move a full-size system unit off the desk and stand it beneath instead—most computer stores sell floor stands, simple brackets that hold a PC upright on its side.

The *monitor* obviously needs to remain on the desk and for many people (especially those engaged in artistic or design-orientated work), the larger it is, the better. The minimum monitor dimension (determined by measuring between diagonally opposite corners of the screen) for comfortable viewing is 14″ and the largest is 21″. Even if you need (and can afford) a large screen it is still possible to reduce the overall space it takes by choosing a swivelling monitor arm or platform—a kind of spring-tension arm which supports the monitor and enables you to 'float' it at any angle just above the desk. This gives you more room on the desk itself, and can also enable you to swing the monitor away, into an alcove or hard against the wall, when you are not using it. It is possible to get hold of almost flat LCD screens which give a crystal-clear picture and no radiation. At the time of writing, however, they are prohibitively expensive and not widely available.

The printer

If you want a good quality printing resource, you cannot avoid the fact that top-of-the-range printers give truly professional results, whilst low-end models just look low-end.

And of course, really good printers are really expensive, and often very large as well. So what should you choose—and do you even need one? It is possible but unlikely that your home office can get away without a printer; if you are exchanging contracts, documents and reports you almost certainly need one, and even less paper-based work benefits from a brief appearance on the page, even if only so that you can read it on the train.

Dot matrix printers

The dot matrix design is the oldest printer type still widely in use, and as they are so much cheaper than laser printers, continue to be popular with small businesses. The way they work is esentially mechanical and electronic. The print head in a dot matrix printer contains short wires or pins (nine or twenty-four), each attached to a small solenoid. As print commands arrive from the computer, a magnetic field is created which forces the pins towards the paper. An ink-coated ribbon lies between the pins and the page, creating the marks which form letters and numbers.

Dot matrix pros	*Dot matrix cons*
• Cheap to buy and maintain.	• Slow.
• 24-pin models produce good quality output.	• Noisy.
• Print on all copies of multi-layer forms.	• Variable reliability relative to laser printers.
	• Difficulty coping with odd or graphics-orientated layouts.

Ink jet printers

Ink jet printers provide an unusual but effective compromise between the cheap clatter of dot matrix printers and the expensive whisper of laser printers. They tend to be small, which is convenient for home users, and capable of surprisingly high quality output. Ink jet printers work by literally firing a jet of ink at the page. Ink is stored in a cartridge to which is attached the print head, a compartment containing tiny nozzles. As print commands arrive, the ink heats up until a tiny droplet is forced through the nozzles onto the paper—a typical character is twenty droplets high by twenty droplets wide.

Ink jet pros	*Ink jet cons*
• Priced nearer to dot matrix than to laser printers.	• Slow.
• Near laser quality print output.	• May require specially coated (and expensive) paper for optimum results.
• Small and compact.	
• Good for colour printing.	

Laser printers
Currently the state-of-the-art printer, the laser printer produces very high quality output quickly and quietly. There is a laser beam within each printer which beams tiny points of light onto a rotating drum, and at the same time paper is pulled along a path called the paper train and charged by an electrical wire—the drum and the paper receive the same type of charge, positive or negative. Once the beam has finished writing, the drum comes into contact with the toner cartridge where its charge draws up particles of toner that stick to the points created by the laser. It then moves to press against the paper, whose charge is stronger than that of the drum, enabling it to draw away the toner onto the paper.

Laser pros	*Laser cons*
• Highest quality output available.	• Expensive! Though prices are dropping all the time.
• Fast.	
• Quiet.	
• High end of technology.	

If you are confident that a printer is not essential, or you do not need to print immediately, or if you really cannot afford one of the quality you need, there are ways to risk doing without a printer entirely. A growing number of high street copy shops and service bureaux will print the contents of a disk for you (for a price), and some public libraries rent laser printers by the hour or by the page. And if you can deal with the ethics, perhaps an office-based friend or spouse can take advantage of the company laser printer.

The fax machine

The convenience of creating an exact copy of the document in your office in an office far away should not be underestimated. In the past five years, most consumers as well as professional people have come to expect the ability, with the companies with which they do business, to send and receive fax transmissions. Certainly, if the local sandwich shop can receive lunch orders by fax, your home office should have one too. You may prefer to deal with paper mail or electronic mail, but it is in your interests to have a fax machine to receive enquiries, instructions and information from clients who may be more (or less) technologically advanced than you.

Whilst the basic fax machine is a relatively simple affair to install and use, it might not be giving you your money's worth, especially if you are looking for a solution that is space- as well as cash-efficient. A better solution might be a combined fax/modem: more technical, it nonetheless costs less than a fax machine and adds the benefits of a modem. Hence, your computer can send and receive fax transmissions along with handling a wide range of other electronic missives, particularly email. You can also print directly from your word processor to the modem when you want to send a fax, and you can print incoming faxes on your computer's printer. If you are feeling brave, it is not that difficult to schedule faxes using the software that comes with a fax/modem. For example, if you have been asked to send a fax at a particular time and know you won't be at your desk in person to do so, you can ask the computer to send it in your absence at the right time. It is also possible to set up groups of fax numbers on your computer and have it send the same fax to everyone in the group at the same time—a much better way to inform clients of your whereabouts or new services. And because the computer sends the fax, received copies never suffer from illegible handwriting, scrunched up pages or dragged lines.

The point to remember about fax documents is that your computer sees them as images rather than text documents, so when it displays a received fax, it does not understand that these are individual letters and words. This means that if you want to use or store the textual information on a received fax, you either have to retype it—or teach your computer to recognise those squiggles. This can be done with optical character recognition (OCR) software which is typically available with scanners but also with some fax software—WinFax Pro from Delrina is a good example.

The modem

If you want to transmit your own data and receive data from other computers, the cheapest and the most universal way is via a modem (MOdulator/DEModulator). A modem is a simple but incredibly useful device to have, and certainly essential to the effective home-worker if you want to do anything more ambitious than make phone calls and travel in order to communicate. It is best to think of the modem as a black box that connects the computer to the phone line. Modern modems can pump data down the phone line at 28,800 bits per second—that's 3,600 bytes every second, provided there is another modem at the far end which can do the same. Modems today are reasonably smart: when you dial a modem, the modems at either end will negotiate with each other to decide the fastest speed they can both sustain, given the types of modem and the phone line's characteristics. The variation between modems is relatively slight and they cost more or less depending mainly on their *baud rate*—the amount of information (measured in bits per second) that they can transmit per unit time.

Although modems are amazingly useful, they are notoriously difficult to get going if you have never come across one before. The terminology surrounding them is mysterious and complex, a fact which owes more to telephone technology than to the modems themselves, but which can be off-putting for newcomers. The good news is that your PC's operating system software, whether Microsoft's Windows 95 or IBM's OS/2 Warp, is now able to work out what kind of modem you have got, and to configure itself accordingly. It is a sad fact that this is still something we cannot take for granted, but most vendors will provide demonstrations and support for their products. Again, buy the best you can and badger the supplier to help you install it and get it running; unreliable or badly set up modems are frustrating and can be damaging to your professionalism.

For more about modems and the online services, see Chapter 4.

The scanner

If your work involves the receipt of a lot of paper—text to proof-read, edit or translate, perhaps—it may be worthwhile investing in a scanner. Essentially, scanners 'read' documents and transfer what they see into the computer. Like fax machines, they cannot normally recognise text except as an image and are normally used to get images and graphics from paper to computer memory. Today, however, optical character recognition software is more widely available and more accurate, and can be used by scanners to translate paper text documents into computer word processing files. Don't be impressed by accuracy rates of less than 98 per cent—although this sounds good, if more than two in every hundred characters are wrong, you are getting at least seven mistakes in a piece of text the size of this paragraph. That's *a lot* of cross-checking and editing.

The CD-ROM drive

Music is just a side-line for the CD-ROM today—they are far more widely (and effectively) used to store information and software. Physically they are tougher than floppy disks as well as flatter and lighter, but they hold up to *six hundred* times as much information. This enormous increase in capacity has made images, sound and video a far more realistic and usable option for the desktop PC, so if your clients have access to CD-ROM it is helpful if you do too. They also work out cheaper: floppies can cost nearly £1.00 each to buy and duplicate, but it costs about one-third of that to press a single CD-ROM. CD-ROM drives have started appearing in new machines, and now you would be hard-pressed to find a new PC without one, although separate units can be bought for older machines. Bear in mind, though, that if you want to use graphics and sound as well as text, you will need a sufficiently powerful machine, video card and sound card to cope. To accommodate this, a lot of computer vendors are now selling carefully packaged 'SOHO Systems', which include all the necessary equipment as standard. If you can start at this level, do: unless you are used to it, it can be a real pain to add cards and drivers to an older system to upgrade it.

What do CD-ROMs add to your machine? Some operating systems and applications are themselves becoming so large (50Mb or more) that their preferred distribution medium is CD-ROM—you need a CD-ROM drive just to install them. Training and instructional materials are also found on CD-ROM now, but the biggest single use of CD-ROMs (apart from games) is reference. Whole libraries of detailed reference information, on almost any subject you care to name, can be bought, stored and searched with ease and speed. Programs such as Microsoft AutoRoute and Map-Vision, which include a full-colour map of the entire United Kingdom as well as some other countries, just would not have been possible before because of the vast quantities of map data involved; few people would have the hard disk space available to store it all. Now they have no need to, since it sits on a single CD-ROM. And do not feel too guilty if the *real* reason why you want a CD-ROM drive is to play games: everyone deserves a little recreation, and once you have the CD-ROM drive the potential for more serious applications is always there. The only disadvantage of the CD-ROM compared to a floppy is that you cannot write your own data to it, but rewritable CD-ROMs are rapidly gaining ground—and that applies to both the drives and the disks themselves.

THE SOFTWARE

However much you spend on it, without the software the hardware is just a shell. Software remains the brain of the computer and the real tool with which you will do the tasks you are committed to, so it is important to get it right. The main priorities should be cost-effectiveness and usability— there is little to be gained by purchasing products that are so difficult to understand and use that you cannot make any progress. On the other hand, it is worth investing a little extra in a product if it is the mainstay of your SOHO career. Programmers, designers (artistic and technical) and illustrators, for example, will have favourite products, perhaps learned over years and representing a storehouse of skill and experience. As it is, there is very little you can think of that someone has not written a program to do— and if there isn't one, there are so many easy-to-use tools around that it is possible, with a little application, to create it yourself.

Although software is extremely sophisticated nowadays, it is worth remembering that, despite its continued power and complexity, it is also much easier to use than ever before. Microsoft Windows, the easy-to-use graphical interface to raw DOS (Disk Operating System), is now the dominant medium for PC users at work and at home and has set standards of usability and 'look and feel' which enable users to buy software which they know will look and behave in a certain way. That is in part because many software companies maintain large usability labs in which people 'off the street' are asked to perform one or more typical tasks. The labs record both the time taken and the way in which the user did the task, and they feed what they have discovered back into the software development process. It is also because the computer press is starting to catch on to the idea of usability, and a few magazines, including the British *PC Magazine*, now have their own usability labs, and score the products for usability as well as performance as part of their reviews.

Hard-working office software

If your skills are more commercial (text or spreadsheets, for example), or even if you do need one specialist product, the SOHO set-up will benefit from a high quality set of office automation software. A word processor, spreadsheet, database and basic graphics capability are essential communication and management tools. The keyword is *suite*: many software manufacturers are actively targeting home-based users by providing fully featured, usable software at much lower prices than are typically available to corporates (although the software suite is also becoming more common in offices now). Software suites are installed as single programs, but include the basic components described above. These work as modules, functioning in isolation but also interacting closely with the other modules in the suite. Thus, for example, you would expect to be able to use name and address information stored in the database to create addressed envelopes in the word processor, or to base pie charts or graphs in the graphics module on data held in the spreadsheet. Popular office suites are Microsoft Office, Lotus SmartSuite and Novell PerfectOffice (ClarisWorks is popular on the Mac). Be aware that most PCs these days come 'bundled' with a suite, so don't spend your money on something that is already installed.

Suites: the key components

The word processor
This is the basic software for creating letters, documents, memos, reports and all written material. You can produce an entire book or long scientific paper using a modern word processor, because it can generate tables of contents, footnotes and endnotes, and even build an index automatically. You can add graphics and charts created in other programs, then see almost instantly what the finished document will look like when it is printed. Of course, just as the possession of a hammer does not make you a carpenter, an all-singing,

all-dancing word processor does not make you a layout artist. Help is at hand. Microsoft and Novell provide what they call *wizards*, *coaches* and *experts* to help you perform certain tasks. For instance, you can hit a button and have the program reformat your document so that it fits into a given number of pages, or get the application to guide you, step by step, through the creation of a table, or laying out a page, or other graphical tasks.

You get a lot of data with a word processor. That is because the software does not just allow you to type words into it—it also has a spell-check dictionary that you can add to, a thesaurus, and lists of words and their usage. That means the program can spell-check your documents, find words with similar meanings for you (useful for crosswords), and even analyse the way you have used the language—then report on the suitability of your writing style for the target audience. The main word processors within suites are Microsoft Word, Novell WordPerfect and Lotus WordPro.

The spreadsheet

A spreadsheet is an electronic version of grid paper, each cell of which can contain a number, text or formula for manipulating the contents of that or other cells. In practice, what you can do with a spreadsheet is manage numbers or text, and build charts, although (as ever) there is a lot more you can do if you are interested. While many of the functions that spreadsheet vendors have added make the products more powerful and give them a far wider range of calculations (it is standard now to be able to perform sophisticated 'what-if' computations), the biggest steps forward have been in the usability and graphical areas. You can now get the software to look at your tables of figures and format them according to a standard, either one that comes with the package or one that you have designed yourself. This allows you to create a common look and feel for all your financial documents—for instance, it is ideal for generating invoices. Main spreadsheets are Microsoft Excel, Lotus 1-2-3 and Novell Quattro Pro.

The presentation package

The easiest way to introduce yourself, your ideas, or your product or service to somebody is to prepare and run a presentation. Presentation software allows you to do just that, by creating a series of visually attractive slides which can be shown, one by one, on your computer, or else linked to a projector. Again, usability is at a premium, with lots of ready-made templates and styles available to get you started. With tips on the maximum number of points you should try to make, the most effective sequence of slides, and stylistic hints popping up, it is relatively simple for even the least artistic business person to create a compelling presentation in moments. The presentation software within popular suites is Microsoft PowerPoint, Lotus Freelance Graphics and Novell Presentations.

The database

Do you need a database? You may not think so, but you have probably already got one. It may look like an address book, or a list of products and their manufacturers, but underlying it is a database. Databases mean different things to different people, but a common thread is the ability to hold large quantities of data—for example, names, addresses and telephone numbers—in a manageable format. The important thing about database software is not so much entering the data as getting it out again in a form that is useful to you. That is where the software earns its keep. Its job is to make the data easy to retrieve, presenting the answers to your questions ('Which of my customers live in the north of England?') in a manner that suits your purposes. Fortunately, like spreadsheets and word processors, databases are more usable now than ever. Look out for Microsoft Access, Lotus Approach and Novell Paradox.

Talking-to-people software

Ironically, communications software remains by far the most difficult to understand and use, and hence the type most people eventually decide to do without. This is unfortunate

since it is by far the most useful and efficient in terms of
getting information of all kinds between yourself and your
client—not to mention getting research information from a
remote database to you in the first place. The reason why
comms software (as it is commonly known) is so prob-
lematic is twofold: firstly, it is only very recently that anyone
except the most specialist computer experts have wanted to
use it, so it has traditionally been designed with expert needs
in mind; and secondly, it encroaches on the mysterious territory of the telephone companies. This raises a whole batch
of new problems, both technical and commercial, which are
not easily resolved by newcomers to this area.

The best way to proceed is to identify exactly what needs
you think you have. Depending on what they are, you can
buy the software to match and avoid unnecessary problems:

Communication need	*Software*
Fax transmission.	Delrina WinFax Pro; other fax software.
Viewing public bulletin boards.	Standard comms package (e.g. Hayes SmartComm).
Commercial research.	WinCIM (interface to CompuServe—see Chapter 4).
Commercial and academic research.	WinCIM and Mosaic or Netscape (graphical interface to the World-Wide Web and Internet resources).
Email to a specific individual or organisation.	Liaise with that individual to specify a product. If there is a corporate link there is probably a standard package already in use. You may need an Internet address.

Email to many different people, speculative mailing, marketing activity.	Mosaic or Netscape access to the Internet; WinCIM access to CompuServe.
Email and file transmission.	The same software as your recipient, ideally! Mature products like CompuServe are well geared to this, otherwise products such as ProComm, PC Anywhere, enable you to dial directly into another PC, provided it is turned on and is running the same software.

Business and money management software

In most cases the standard office software described above will be adequate for your business management needs. The more sophisticated products (particularly Microsoft Office) include a range of templates, or ready-made processes (macros), which make time and financial management easier. Most spreadsheets now include, for example, some sort of budgeting or planning capability whilst word processors come with ready-made invoice designs.

Nonetheless, that should not blind you to the power of software designed specifically to take on these tasks. Manufacturers realise that not everyone who needs to organise their money is an accountant, and this is particularly true for people setting up a small business at home. *Quicken*, by Intuit, is a finance management package specifically for home and small-business users and assumes no specialist financial knowledge. On the contrary, it includes a full range of tutorials to get you going and uses no accounts terminology—indispensable if you need to keep a close eye on income and expenditure.

Personal Information Managers (PIMs)

PIMs act as computerised diaries plus a whole lot more. Typically, you will find diary facilities, an address database, planner, scheduler and memo writing resource, all geared to managing your time and resources efficiently. The problem PIMs have always had (however good they are) is one of portability—most people need to check their appointments and addresses when they are away from their PC, and while some PIMs (and their information) can be transferred via download to a notebook PC, they have never been able to compete with pen and paper for sheer convenience. Nowadays, however, palmtop computers are becoming the modern PIM—tiny computers with PIM-type software built in, which offer the portability of a diary. Which you go for is really a matter of personal preference. There is a good range of products for managing your time (TaskTimer by Time/system), your appointments, and also more specific software which will control your mailing labels, for example. Not all of these capabilities will be necessary or affordable, so choose what is obviously important or useful for your particular needs. It is as well to be aware of niche products, however, since needs can change and it may become more cost-effective for you to start (or stop) using a particular product at some point.

Contact management software

Related to but more specialised than PIM software, contact management software (ACT!, Tracker, Contact Pro) stores names and addresses like a normal database, but also allows you to record times and details of phone calls, conversations, meetings and appointments. When a client calls, simply type in his name and you are presented with details of the last few talks you had with him, plus information about who agreed to do what, whether it was done and what the next stage should be. The idea behind these products is that you are always on the ball and can get the most out of introductions and chats at every level by storing key facts and figures.

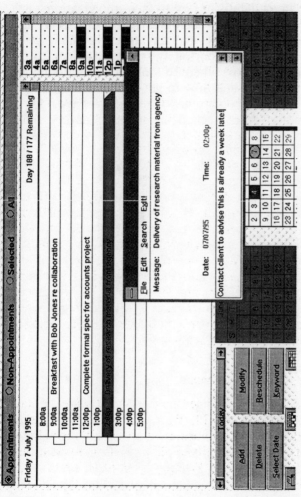

Using some sort of diary or time manager to schedule meetings, appointments and work periods goes a long way to reducing hassle and stress. Several time management techniques can be employed to maintain levels of motivation, keep important information uppermost in your mind and enable you to feel that goals are being achieved.

The good news is that some of the best contact management packages are DOS-based rather than Windows. The software is commonly used when your attention is elsewhere—the telephone, contract details or face to face conversation—and a decision or response is needed quickly. Keystrokes are still quicker than mouse clicks, and an attractive interface is meaningless if it grinds laboriously from one screen to the next. Users need to know where to look on screen to get the information they need and how to get different information in a single gesture. If you are lucky enough to have a lot of clients, computerised contact management is a very smart move.

3 Getting Started: How and Where to Buy a Computer

In this chapter we shall be looking at what you can expect a PC to do, what kinds of software are available for the job, which products fit into those categories, and how to buy them. As you would expect, purchasing a PC is a compromise between budget availability and the possibly conflicting requirements of the different uses to which it will be put. Finally, we shall discuss the vexed question of which operating system to use: don't panic if you are not sure what an operating system is: if you are interested you can read that section; if not, it is not essential.

WHICH APPLICATION SOFTWARE?

Here is a crucial maxim that dates from the days when there were lots of kinds of computer you could choose from rather than just one or two, but which still holds true: *sort out what you want to do with the computer before you even think about what kind of software and hardware to buy*. The single most common cause of frustration and wasted money is thinking of the computer as a piece of hardware rather than as a tool for running applications—that is, software. It can result in buying a computer and then discovering that it is unsuitable—either it does not have enough memory or disk space, or the processor is not powerful enough, or it needs an additional adaptor card or peripheral device attached to it. And upgrading is more expensive than buying the right PC in the first place, so if all the money has been spent on the

PC itself, it will shunt the cost way beyond your original budget.

Only once you know what kinds of jobs you are going to ask the computer to do—that is, what kinds of software you are going to run—can you start making sensible, informed decisions about what kind of hardware you need. That is why we shall discuss software first—and why you should be thinking about it first, too.

Choosing software

If all you need is functional office productivity software— word processors, spreadsheets and databases being the big three —the choice of software is generally simple: either you buy one of the so-called 'office suites' from one of the big three software houses—Lotus, Microsoft or Novell—or you buy separate applications from different vendors. The contents of suites vary, but all will provide you with the basics to get you going, such as a word processor, a spread-sheet, and a personal organiser. In addition, you may get a database, a presentation package and an electronic mail sys-tem, depending on which option you choose. Suites are discussed in much more detail in Chapter 2.

What you gain from buying a suite is the knowledge that the various software components are designed to work together, and that you will not have to plough through an individual installation process for each of them. You also get one each of the major types of software you are likely to need. Buying software in this way satisfies most people and is likely to provide a much better deal than you could get only a few years ago, when each application on its own might cost around £500. Now, many users find it worthwhile to buy a software suite for much less than that simply to acquire one or two of its modules, and regard the rest as free extras. You can also be reasonably sure that almost every feature in each of the applications that you think you might need (and probably another two or three dozen that you don't) is in the box, as the leading suites consist of the top-selling packages of the biggest software vendors.

So for instance, Microsoft Office includes Word, Power-Point (a presentation graphics application) and the spreadsheet Excel; the Professional edition adds Access, a database management application. Even if you use only the word processor most of the time and need the occasional use of a spreadsheet, it is still going to be worthwhile buying a suite. Better still, with many PCs these days, you are likely to get a suite bundled in with the hardware.

On the other hand, the monolithic, everything-in-the-one-box approach has its drawbacks. You are more than likely to say yes to every prompt the office suite's install routine offers you and install the lot, and only afterwards wonder where up to 100 megabytes of your disk space disappeared to. Uninstalling pieces of this software might prove more hazardous than you thought, and can lead to you having to reinstall the lot just to retain the bits you want. You might also find that, while the word processor suits you, the spreadsheet does not, but you will be stuck with it because the cost of buying in something new is usually not worth it. What is more, if you find that you do not use half the software in the box, it can lead to the uncomfortable feeling that you have paid money for something you do not require.

Be aware that you may still need specialist software for special requirements: for instance, if you are planning to convert paper documents into an electronic form so that you can store, manipulate and search them in future, you will need an optical character recognition (OCR) application as well. Even more specialist software, such as the image editors and creators used by graphic artists, or professional desktop publishing packages, can be expensive, mainly because the economies of scale do not apply as strongly in this area, and also because the assumption is that you are buying a tool for a particular commercial purpose.

Either way, while buying software is less of a leap into the dark than it was as a result of the common look and feel imposed by Microsoft Windows, it is always advisable to get some hands-on experience of the product before you spend money: try before you buy. Trying before you buy applies particularly if you are going to need specialist software which may not get reviewed in magazines that often, and with which many dealers—or other experts to whom you might turn, such as knowledgeable friends and acquaintances—may not be very familiar.

Check also that the software works the way you want to work. For instance, you are likely to want to process similar types of document each time you use the software, so look for a package that can automate as much of the process as possible, so that you only have to set up the job once. The setting up of an automated job ought to be both pain-free and intuitive, and if it is, that will encourage you to tackle more complex tasks when the challenge presents itself. In the long term, that will expand the range of opportunities that you and your business can tackle.

When you want to try out software before buying, to make absolutely sure that it does what you want, your friendly local dealer becomes invaluable. See the section below on dealers.

Do you have a licence for that software?
As with hardware, while the cheapest software prices are usually to be found inside the pages of the fattest PC magazines, if you buy this way you do not get a chance to look at the merchandise first. What is more, you will find that the process of opening the package and extracting the disks from their paper envelope has committed you to the terms of the software licence, although you only know exactly what those terms are once the package has been opened. Even though in practice most of those terms and conditions are roughly the same and hardly impact on normal usage of the software, they might prevent you from installing it on two separate PCs, even though you will only be using one of them at any time. You are rarely allowed legally to run the same software for two or more people's simultaneous use. Worse still, the product will have become unreturnable in the eyes of the direct, off-the-page software vendor. A good dealer, however, will allow you to check out the software first, particularly if you have demonstrated good faith by not rushing off to get the cheapest price after having exploited his or her facilities.

On the question of software licences, while the exact terms vary from product to product, you will need to be aware that you rarely buy software outright. Instead, purchasing the goods entitles you to use the software in the manner prescribed. In other words, if you buy a word processor for a single user, you are not entitled to install it on every PC in the office—unless of course you are the only user of that software. The reason is that, unlike almost every other type of product, software is totally reproducible: you can copy the disks and the result is just as good as the original. If you need three copies of a package—in other words, if there are three users—then you must buy three copies, or three licences, or you are breaking the law. In general, you can usually install a product for use by one individual on two separate machines at different times without legal ramifications, the classic example being a software package that is used at work and at home. Check the individual licence terms, though.

HARDWARE: SETTING PRIORITIES

You should by now have a reasonable idea of the kinds of use to which you would like to put your new PC, but it is important to firm up exactly what you will demand from the machine, and which uses are dispensable. That will help you determine priorities when the computer salesperson on the other end of the phone starts offering you options, such as a discount on a PC without a CD-ROM drive, for instance. It will also mean that when you start looking through a fat computer magazine which seems to consist almost exclusively of advertisements and those irritating bits of cardboard, you'll have a clearer idea of the kinds of machine which you can automatically reject.

It is rather like buying a car. You would not buy a Mercedes as a nippy city runabout, or a Rover Metro as a fast, motorway-gobbling, luxury vehicle. In the same way, there is no point in getting a massively powerful machine with a huge hard disk, loads of memory and bucket-loads of accessories if all you want to do is write words and do a little light accounting work. On the other hand, you would find it pretty frustrating to end up with a low-specification PC that included the minimum requirements for running Windows if you were expecting to produce graphic images or edit digital video.

While those two examples sit at opposite ends of the specification spectrum and there is, of course, room between them for a machine that can do a bit of both, there is another element to add to the equation: obsolescence. The computer business is notorious for the speed with which the technology evolves—rather like watching flowers unfurl using time-lapse photography. Each advance is a step towards better performance, or a new feature that either makes the machine more usable or gives it access to a new set of applications.

PCs become obsolete very quickly. The life-cycle of the latest machine is likely to be up to six months, sometimes less. After that, another internal piece of PC—such as a motherboard, graphics card or disk controller—comes along, and the manufacturer decides it adds enough performance or features to the original PC's specification to justify calling it a new model. It will probably be the same price or cheaper, so the machine sitting on the shelf six months after you bought yours is unlikely to resemble it internally, even if the case looks the same, the name-badge aside. Everyone buying a PC is in the same dilemma: do I buy now or wait until the price has dropped or the vendor has added another desirable feature or widget? The answer has to be that you bite the bullet and buy now, because if you wait six months, the magazines will be full of articles about what is coming over the horizon in another six months' time, and you will be no further on—and you will have been without the use of a PC for half a year.

Remember that you can choose a PC for running standard office-type Windows applications (see p. 55 for an explanation of Windows) without too much difficulty provided you tell the salesperson what you want it for and how much you are prepared to spend. The three main indicators of PC power that you should look at hardest are the processor speed, the amount of memory, and the amount of hard disk space.

Multimedia

The latest popular home purchase is the multimedia PC, a beast which, in addition to running software, will also store and play back digitised sound and video. On the software side, Windows comes with most of the basic tools you need to get started. But with the advent of video sources as diverse as the Internet and the digital camcorder, you will require special tools for doing such things as digital video and sound editing. From a hardware perspective, multimedia machines include at least a CD-ROM drive and a sound card. If your hardware or software requirements are more specialised than this, they are beyond the scope of this book and you would do best to seek advice from specialist publications or consultants.

The CD-ROM drive will be able to play CD-ROMs, which look exactly like CDs for the very good reason that they use exactly the same technology, except that they are used to store computer data rather than music. Computer CD players are similar to the one to be found in your living-room, but with some additions. For a start, they are much more precise because, while your ears will not hear a few dropped bits from a piece of music from a less-than-pristine CD, the PC will not be as tolerant of missing bits from a program.

Many of them also rotate the disk two, three, four or even six times as fast as your CD player—although they can still play a music CD at standard speed if required to do so. The faster the disk spins, the quicker you get your data off it, and that can be particularly important for sound and video. If the computer is displaying a moving video, it needs to be fed with enough data to display 25 frames every second. That is a lot of data, and if it has to wait because the CD-ROM drive cannot deliver the data fast enough, you will see drop-outs or jerky images. Spin the CD-ROM faster, and the rate at which that data can be streamed off goes up in proportion. A

CD-ROM's big advantage is that it will safely store up to 650 megabytes of data—the exact length of sound or video you can store depends on the compression method used. If used to store raw text, it will house some 260,000 A4 pages.

You may well want a CD-ROM drive for a purpose unconnected with multimedia. The CD-ROM has become a popular medium, easy to carry around and cheap because it is mass-produced. In fact, so cheap has it become that software vendors are finding that sending out floppy disks, with their extra weight, unreliability and inconvenience factor, is costing them much more. As a result, many major software companies sell their applications today on one or more CD-ROMs, Corel Draw, and Novell's PerfectOffice suite of programs. See Chapter 2 for further discussion of this issue.

This trend is on the increase, and if you think you may want to upgrade your software at some point you can save yourself money (because the CD-ROM versions are often cheaper) and time (because you don't have to shovel floppy disks into the drive every three minutes) by buying a PC with a working CD-ROM drive to start with. Not doing so will save you about £100 or so, but if you later find you need the drive, installation could be fiddly.

Sound cards come in two main flavours: 8-bit and 16-bit. The 16-bit variety allows programs to reproduce a much wider range of sounds, rather than the somewhat limited electronic weebling you might well associate with music on the PC. For general business purposes and for the occasional game, the point to look for is compatibility with the Creative Labs' product, the Soundblaster, as almost all applications that make use of high quality sound are Soundblaster-compatible.

How much to pay

After you have decided what kind of PC you need and what software you want to run on it, the next issue is likely to be the price. The temptation is simply to go for the cheapest—after all, a PC is a fairly hefty investment, and you need it for your business. Why pay more than you have to?

As you would expect, however, it is not as simple as that. Both the number of features and the quality of a PC are closely yoked to its price. At the bottom end of the market prices are low and you are more likely to be able to argue for a better price, but you are also more likely to find machines that have been put together in a hurry. That can result in such faults as a hard disk that does not appear to work, which could be the consequence of the vendor not checking that the cables have been pushed home firmly enough. The hard disk cable then comes loose in transit, so when the machine arrives at its final destination it will not work. The same can be true of chips, particularly memory modules that the vendors will have fitted themselves, as opposed to the soldered-on chips that were present when the manufacturer bought the motherboard (a motherboard is the PC's main circuit board). In either case, after paying several hundred pounds for a product, you cannot be expected to have to take the machine apart to make it work, even if two minutes of jiggling all the cables firmly into their sockets would do the trick. It is likely to take at least a few days to get the machine back to where you bought it from and get it returned in working condition, during which time you are without a PC.

The good news is that PCs are much more likely to fail at the start of their lives. So if a PC is working when it arrives and carries on for the first day or so, it will probably stay that way for a good while—two or three years at least and probably much longer. The general trend in the PC business is towards higher component reliability, especially as manufacturers build more and more functions onto fewer and fewer chips. It is also fair to say that most PCs work when they arrive and carry on working; just be prepared for a higher probability of a fault, most likely a minor one, if price is your sole guide in the buying process.

Paying more—the comfort factor?
The alternative is to pay a higher, fixed price to a larger vendor. This route offers the comfort factor that they are less likely to quibble about repairs and machines that are dead on arrival. Such manufacturers also tend to do more testing and to

use higher quality components with a better specification—although there is little evidence that they are any more or less likely to fail. What you pay for is a high build quality and better design—which could mean the difference between having to semi-dismantle a PC to install new memory modules, and simply lifting the lid and slotting them in.

You will get better documentation too. Smaller PC vendors cannot afford to have manuals specially printed to their own specification, which will offer a seamless guide to the entire product you have just bought, as bigger vendors do. Paying a lower price means that you will find there are separate booklets for each of the components that go to make up the PC—motherboard, CD-ROM drive, sound card and DOS, for instance—and if you need help or something goes wrong, the vital pieces of information may well be scattered across several of the booklets, each of which will deliver different levels of helpfulness.

LOOKING FOR BARGAINS

Don't let any of the above stop you looking for bargains. In the pages of the local newspaper, or one of the more serious computer magazines, you can find bargains. In particular, it is worth looking for machines that are a generation or two behind what is known as the leading edge. So look for what is new and jump back two or three clock speeds: for instance, if a 133MHz Pentium is new, then a 66MHz Pentium will be cheap.

Stop press!

The best place to look, at least at first, is the specialist press. Magazines such as *Computer Shopper*, *PC Direct* and *Personal Computer World* contain hundreds of pages of advertisements put up by PC manufacturers and software vendors who sell their wares directly off the page. All aim to tempt you to buy. The PC business is a fiercely competitive market, and a read through even a month's worth of three of those magazines will give you an instant feel for what is and is not a good price. If you do decide to buy a PC directly from the manufacturer, knowledge can save you money, as you will be able to pit one vendor against another. Do not take no for an answer, and do not deal with anyone who refuses to haggle: there are plenty more fish in the sea.

However, it is often the case that prices agree with each other within a few pounds. So is this a cartel? Probably not. There are two main reasons: because the costs of running such operations are about the same, and because the places where the advertisers bought the hardware or software in the first place—not necessarily the original software house—are actually the same, as are the prices they paid. But beware as, in general, the cheaper the price, the less you can expect in the way of support and services. So if you want something a little more complex such as a network, don't buy direct unless you know exactly what you want.

Don't expect to get a 20-minute explanation of the feature set of each product you are considering, particularly when buying software, which tends to be more complex. Nor will you get much, if any, after-sales service if you decide you do not want a software product—whether because it does not work properly or because it does not suit you. The terms of the licence almost always include a disclaimer for any damage caused by the software—there is no guarantee that it will work the way it is supposed to and there is little if anything that you, the user, can do about it. The reason for this is largely because there is almost no way in which software authors can guarantee that software will be totally bug-free. Alas, even computer programs written for aircraft control systems or military purposes, which are seriously life-threatening should they fail, and which have hundreds of times as much bug-hunting time put into them, have bugs. The odds of this not being true of your word processor are minuscule.

One more consideration. If you buy hardware from a company that is geographically close to you, you will be able to take the machine back if it fails rather than having to go through the hassle of packing it up and arranging collection and delivery. You might even be able to talk to the person who bolted the machine together in the first place.

Reading between the lines

In between the ads in the fatter magazines you may encounter some editorial. Read with caution. It consists largely of journalists waxing enthusiastic about the latest products, most of which would take a month or more of their salaries to buy. The reason why the press gets worked up about the latest thing and leaves older products behind is simple. The magazine market is just as competitive as the PC business it serves. Journalists vie to get the latest widget because they fear being scooped by their rivals. They are spoiled by having almost unfettered access to the latest technology, to the extent that many tend to lose sight of the fact that most buyers of small or home office PCs cannot justify paying top prices for the very latest product. It is also a lot easier for them to get hold of brand-new product than older equipment that has been out for a while, or that has been superseded because the manufacturers have brought out an upgraded version. Note that these are the same manufacturers who advertise in that magazine, who want editorial coverage of the new products they are advertising, on which they will make the largest margin.

You can get extra value from the press, though, as many magazines run comparative review features which pit products—hardware and software—of a particular type against each other. Often less news-driven than the stand-alone reviews, they can be valuable in that they show you what is currently on the market, and you can often gain a clearer idea of the criteria by which judgements about the products are made. It is even possible to phone the magazine to find out more, but don't be surprised if you get short shrift, especially at press time, as most magazine journalists see their primary job as getting the magazine out, not answering technical queries.

SUPPORT YOUR LOCAL DEALER

Your second port of call should be the high street computer dealer. Few and far between, if you find one that suits you, spend your money there. A dealer makes his or her living out of selling everything from a cable you suddenly find you need late one Saturday afternoon, to your first word processing package. He or she will spend far more time with you than anyone else in the business, and will be happy to sit down and discuss your needs with you, and guide you towards the products that fit your requirements. The dealer will hold your hand as you try out the software and discuss what kinds of hardware you are going to need to run it on.

Just as importantly, the dealer can be a mine of information about what is coming up, and whether a piece of software or hardware is a good buy. Without assiduous scouring of computer magazines, it is not always easy to tell if a product is about to be superseded and replaced by something that delivers exactly the feature you've been looking for. Dealers can do all that researching for you, and make it all work together. If you get the advice and products you need, you are a happy customer, and they stand to make more money that way. If they won't help, don't go there.

What you are unlikely to get from a dealer is the cheapest price, and it is unreasonable to expect it. Certainly, some dealers will offer to match magazine page prices, but any high street computer dealer who is offering that sort of discount across the board is either buying the goods through an unauthorised channel which is unlikely to last, or is not very good at business: it costs a lot more to run a shop than to advertise in a magazine from warehouse premises. Why do you care? First of all, you want that dealer to be there in six or 12 months' time when you next need advice. And if you are running a business, you should seriously consider whether price is the single most important criterion for choosing a channel for product purchasing: good information, guidance and expertise can be priceless in time savings alone, never mind the frustration factor.

The PC warehouse

Companies such as PC World—the best known—have set up out-of-town stores where you can go along to touch and feel the goods before buying. Prices may not be the keenest but at least you can see what you are getting. They have also usually got a good range of software on show, although you will probably find a better price in the pages of a magazine. Help, too, can sometimes be hard to find.

SECOND-HAND PCs

Second-hand PCs are a very mixed bunch. When hunting them down, the temptation to compromise is great, but there are some areas where it is just not worth it. You might think that a fairly old computer that is very cheap is a bargain. But the chances are that even if it has the processing power to run Windows, it will have neither enough memory nor a big enough hard disk to store and run today's programs. Even if you plan to upgrade it, new components and old PCs often do not mix well.

It is possible that an older PC—one that is more than three or four years old—will not accept today's slot-in memory modules (known as SIMMs), as modern machines have moved from 36-pin SIMMs to 72-pin SIMMs. Older machines may also not accept SIMMs that have anything larger than 1Mb memory chips in them: these are now a very expensive way of buying memory as they are not made in any great quantity, unlike 4Mb or 16Mb chips.

You may also find that adding a faster processor may make very little difference, because the bottleneck in performance is elsewhere in the machine; this is often the case.

Hard disks too have got bigger—the price of a 1Gb disk has fallen to the price of a 250Mb disk two or three years earlier. They have also become more standardised in the way in which they interface with the hard disk controller—that is the circuitry which manages the storage of your files on the hard disk. But an older PC may well not be totally compatible with a new hard disk, with the result that, even if it appears at first to work, files may eventually become corrupted so that you lose data.

All of which is not intended to put you off buying second-hand: it is just that PCs are technically complex, so it is advisable to take with you someone who knows what he or she is looking for. Be aware too that PC prices are continually falling: £1,000 today buys a PC that is of an order of magnitude more powerful than could have been bought with the same amount of money three or four years ago.

Second-hand software, too, may be a bargain or it may not. It is hard to make blanket judgements because it depends on the package, but you are likely to find that technical support for older software is more difficult if not impossible to get, and if you do not have the original box or at least the registration documents or some proof of purchase, you will get short shrift from the technical support line. Perhaps the biggest drawbacks are that it is unlikely to support modern hardware features, such as a fast, cheap GDI printer; that it may not conform to modern custom and practice about the user interface (the way the program presents itself and how you make it work); and that if you have to exchange files with others, if they are running a more modern package you may not be able to read their files.

WHICH OPERATING SYSTEM?

It is all very well to say that you decide what you want to do with a PC and then go and buy one. The problem is that we all want to do a mixture of things—including playing games—and that, if you have never had one before, you do not know what kind of other things you might find for it to do. And it can be frustrating if you discover that you cannot, for instance, access the Internet at the most economical speed without buying a new card to plug into the PC's expansion slots.

Perhaps the first issue is to decide whether you want to run Windows. Microsoft's Windows has transformed the PC, which until recently lagged behind the much prettier Macintosh in terms of usability—in other words, what the screen looks like, how information is presented on the screen, and how clear the options are.

Windows is Microsoft's biggest-selling product, which boosted the company into a multi-billion-dollar business.

Effectively the face or personality of the computer, Windows uses framed boxes (windows) on the screen to enclose icons which in turn represent programs or documents. It assigns your programs into logical groups—or the groups you put them in—so that you can, for instance, put programs and documents that relate to a specific project in one group. A mouse on your desk is connected to the PC with a cable, and dragging it around the desk results in the movement of a pointer on the screen. You run a program by moving the pointer to an icon, and double-clicking on its icon with the left mouse button; double-clicking is clicking twice in quick succession in the same place.

The result of Windows' success is that almost all new programs are designed to run with it—see Chapter 2 for more details of Windows software and what it does. The benefits it confers are such that you should do without it and use just DOS only if your budget is very limited indeed.

If you decide to run only DOS, you will be running mostly older software, for which the software company that made it may well have either abandoned support or disappeared; if things go wrong you will be on your own. There are high quality, DOS-only programs available that act as partial replacements for Windows. They include PC Tools for DOS (sold by Symantec) and XTREE Gold (also sold by Symantec). Such packages allow you to organise your PC and run your application programs without having to type commands in at the DOS prompt, but you do not get as much information on the screen because they are almost all limited to 80 characters across by either 25 or 50 rows down. The upside to all this is that you can pick up very cheaply old PCs that cannot run Windows but make perfectly adequate DOS machines—and we shall explore how to go about this later on (see p. 74).

Another alternative to Windows is IBM's rival product, OS/2 Warp. From the user's perspective it works in much the same way as Windows—it allows you to run Windows programs using the mouse, pointer, icons and so on. It is technically more advanced than Windows and offers many more features—you can tailor the way it works to a much greater extent, and it does not crash as often as Windows tends to—but it needs twice as much memory as Windows 3.11 does, making the PC more expensive.

On the other hand, Warp's memory needs are about the same as Windows 95, so if your PC is running that, you can run Warp. The disadvantage of Warp is that few people use it, which means that getting technical support from hardware and software vendors is harder, and there are not very many software packages which are designed to run on OS/2.

However, your PC is in fact unlikely to arrive without either a copy of Windows 3.11 or its more powerful successor, Windows 95, already installed and running.

TEN TIPS FOR BUYING A SOHO SYSTEM
(from *Computer Shopper* (USA))

1 **Don't skimp**. Stick to a realistic budget, but remember that this purchase may be the most important capital expenditure you make in business. It is likely that it will have to last a few years, too. Compromise on your system now, and you will compromise in your business.

2 As far as possible, **buy from a single source**, even if it costs a little more to stay with one vendor. Shopping around is good up to a point, especially for major purchases, but it can also cost you precious time. So always weigh your savings against your own efforts. And if you ever need service or support, you will have to deal with only one vendor.

3 **Get DOS and Windows pre-installed**. It is hard to find a system without this, but insist on it. You will save time and aggravation, and be ready to get started when the boxes arrive. Be sure, too, that you demand the installation disks and manuals for these products. Some vendors will not provide them unless you ask.

4 **Get a quality printer**. Your printed communication is an ambassador for your business, so spend the money to look good. An inkjet is the minimum acceptable quality for business correspondence. A personal laser printer is better.

5 **Add as many communication functions to your PC as you can afford**. Using your computer for fax, email, voice mail and other communications makes you more efficient.

6 **Get a CD-ROM drive pre-installed**. Whether it will be used for researching databases, training you to use your computer and new software, or just to make the installation of large operating systems and applications quick and easy, a CD-ROM is a business-computer necessity. And don't buy it separately unless you must. CD-ROMs are not simple installations—no matter what your vendor promises.

7 Consider a **tape backup** or other high-speed backup storage device. If your business is on the computer, then you should have a daily plan to protect the data from loss or damage.

8 **Make sure your computer order is in stock**, or, if it isn't, that it will be delivered within an acceptable period of time. Cancel the order if you wait longer than promised. Your business cannot afford to sit idle while you wait for a computer.

9 **Check the vendor's warranty and support terms** carefully. If on-site service is promised, find out who decides the conditions of dispatching—you or the vendor. And make sure technical support is available during your working hours; 24-hour support is common, but it might not be live support at all hours. Find out. At minimum, be sure your vendor has a part-replacement policy with next-day delivery.

10 Get all the details of your order in writing, and **never pay by cash or cheque**. Always use a credit card. Make sure the vendor also provides a money-back no-questions-asked guarantee of at least 30 days. And enquire whether the guarantee includes hidden costs like a restocking fee. Find out if you have to pay for dispatch, as well, in the event of a return.

4 Online: The Brave New World of the Home-worker

There is a lot of hype these days about cyberspace, that 'world-wide web of computers linked together', but with just a small investment in both time and money you could have the whole system at your fingertips. Once you have mastered the technology, you could turn your phone line into a conduit for information of every type, from all over the world.

No matter how complex the systems that make it all happen, the end user—you and I—must be able to manage it all simply, in a way that makes the whole thing useful. You don't have to be a rocket scientist to drive your car, and the same applies, or should apply, to computers. They should be simple to use and allow you to manage them in an intuitive manner, no matter where they are in relation to you. Alas, they have not yet reached that state of grace, but things are a lot better than they were and this extra ease of use, combined with the relative cheapness of the equipment, means that more ordinary people are using the technology for real business reasons. This in turn means that there is a greater demand for and supply of a wide range of information.

There is a welter of data available to help you get an edge over your competition, but that's not all. As well as being able to discover the latest developments in almost any field that is relevant to you, thanks to the huge number of academic institutions online, you are also enriched by contact with many people whom you might otherwise not have met. In fact you may never meet them in the flesh, but only in the virtual, online world. Access to online information also allows you to respond quickly to new events in your particular market, and it is cheaper in the long run than buying information—particularly market research which is essential to the success of any business. And there could be intangible benefits, too. Using, and being seen to use, the latest technology shows your clients that you are keeping pace with modern developments. If you are online, you are even more impressive.

If you are still unconvinced, think about the telephone. In its early days, few thought that it would become an almost universal means of communication—in the developed world at least. It was too complex and expensive. That changed when the number of people connected to it reached critical mass, whereupon it became highly desirable to be hooked into the telephone network. In that transition period, those who used the phone had an edge because they could communicate instantly, unlike those who were limited to pen and paper. We are now approaching critical mass in electronic communications, and over the next five years are likely to see an explosion in the numbers of people using computers to communicate.

Let's look at some of the main services and technologies that make such a world possible, and discuss how to get the most out of them.

ONLINE SERVICES

You must by now have heard of the Internet and have an idea of what it is: a vast worldwide network of over two million computers, most of which allow public access to all or part of the databases of information that they contain. They also include bulletin boards (Usenet groups) where you can discuss everything from sex to scientology, as well as recreational uses such as multi-user games. Most Internetted computers allow you to browse through their lists of files and transfer files from there to your own computer—a process known as downloading. And you can exchange electronic mail (email) with anyone in the world who has an email address—and the list of people who include such addresses on their business cards is growing too.

Until recently, the process of accessing the Internet was arcane and expensive, but today there is an explosively growing list of companies offering access at reasonable rates: your modem dials their modem, the two connect, you enter your name and password, and you are linked to the world's biggest collection of data. Better news still is that there is now a free piece of software, Netscape, that eliminates the awkward methods and most of the jargon required to get onto the Internet.

Netscape links you up to the World-Wide Web, which is the pretty face of the Internet. The most useful thing about it is that it runs under Windows, and provides a 'point and shoot' way of getting at any kind of information. Being graphical, it can handle pictures, sound, video—just about anything that can be turned into digital bits—as well as the pure text to which more traditional tools are limited.

Costs

The good news is that the upfront cost is fairly cheap. You do not need heavy-duty hardware, and the only accessory you must have is a modem. One that will cope with most uses can cost little more than £100. The bad news is that every second you are online costs you money. The least you will pay is the phone connect charge, as the telephone company treats modem calls exactly the same as standard voice calls. Then there are online charges levied by the service to which you connect: in general the rule is that the more useful the data to which you are getting access, the more it will cost. Accessing a database of newspaper cuttings or extracts from legal journals can be costly, whereas logging into a service that provides mostly files which are in the public domain will be much cheaper. Bulletin boards are largely free and so are useful places on which to cut your teeth.

Services that charge do so according to the length of time you are connected to them, while others may add extra charges if you use an additional service, such as a search of newspaper text. The pernicious practice of charging you more if you connect using a fast modem is dying out, partly because fast modems are now so cheap that most people use them, and partly because it can be hard for users to work out whether it's cheaper to dial in using a slow link that incurs the cost of a longer phone call, or a fast link with a shorter call.

The details of how the technologies work are beyond the scope of this book. You should grab a technical book or magazine if you want to delve deeper, but you will need to know where some of the nuts and bolts are so that you can tweak a system to suit your needs and fix things if something should go wrong.

The Internet

The Internet, made up of millions of computers all over the world, and even more millions of users, is a huge subject on its own. Here our aim is merely to explain what it is, what you can expect from it, and how to get onto it. When it comes to the Internet, beware of hype. The numbers involved (whether we are talking about traffic in bytes, the number of users, the number of computers, or the number of messages) are enormous. Thirty million users, maybe three million computers, untold millions of connections—all human life is there.

That is its main attraction: you can find scientific papers on the most obscure subjects, pictures taken by the Hubble Space Telescope, news and sport from the *Daily Telegraph*'s online service, and information on a welter of products, from Californian pizzas to jewellery to office equipment. And you can buy things. The main problems with the Internet are tracking down the data that interests you, and the security aspects of online commerce—there is almost none.

There are also discussion areas on the Internet called *newsgroups*. Here you can find discussions on almost every topic, from the day's news to biology to games, and they can be entertaining and mentally stimulating—but they can also be a huge drain on your time; it is probably not economical to get too closely involved in them, at least until you are more accustomed to the idioms adopted online.

A word on one of the misconceptions that have built up around the Internet. If you think you are likely to come across weirdos touting peculiar sexual practices and the like, please don't worry. You are as likely to come across something you don't like the look of there as you are in other aspects of your life: in other words, if you look for something hard enough, you will probably eventually find it. If you don't, you almost certainly won't.

The World-Wide Web

The WWW is a fast-growing group of Internet computers that can deliver their information in a graphical fashion, which makes such Internet sites much more friendly and easy to use. What does a WWW service on the Internet look like? That is up to the provider, for there is no standard enforced. Some are better-looking than others, although the standard is improving daily as more commercial concerns hang out their signs on the Internet: they want their WWW pages to look presentable when you first encounter their organisation.

Essentially, a WWW page consists of text and images that are displayed within the window of your browser. The most common elements you will find are an image at or near the top that opens the page, headlines introducing the subjectmatter, followed by either the meat of the information that interests you or a menu of further information which that service offers. More and more common is the addition of sound and moving video to WWW documents, so if you anticipate doing lots of online work, when specifying your computer bear in mind that it may need that capability.

At the heart of the WWW's flexibility and ease of use is a device known as *hypertext linking*. Hypertext is like an index. Known as a link, the index entry is there in front of you, embedded in the current document, but it is active. So rather than having to go and find the page or address to which the index entry points, clicking on a link cuts out a step and takes you there directly. A link looks like a piece of

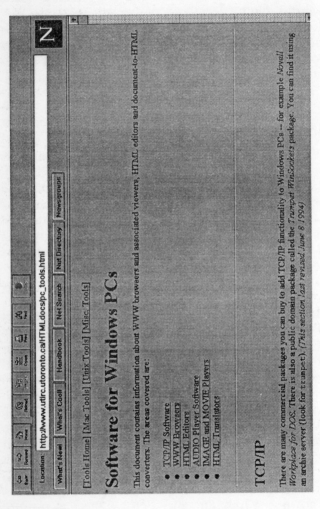

The World-Wide Web (WWW) is one of the fastest and most accessible areas of the Internet because of its graphical interface and ease of navigation. The page illustrated provides information on the software required to browse the Web and ultimately build your own page.

highlighted text (usually shown as underlined blue text) and when you move the standard Windows arrow cursor over it, the cursor changes into an upright pointer. When you activate a link, you don't have to know where the information behind it is physically located, and you jump from the document you were viewing into a new one. The system allows you either to follow a train of thought, or to wander around aimlessly—you have to supply the discipline here.

For example, if you want details of provisions for disabled people in different countries, you might find a service that has an overview, with the names of the various countries on which the service has data highlighted as links. If you click on a link, you access the details you were after, but then you might find a link pointing to details of that country's transport policies, for example. Follow that link and, unless you are single-minded, a few links later you will be avidly reading through a treatise on pre-war photography. On the other hand, if you are disciplined about it you can drill down to the kind of information that might take you hours or even days to unearth when searching through paper archives.

If you want to find information of any kind, using Windows-based World-Wide Web (WWW) browser software, the best way to start is to connect to a computer that specialises in gathering details about the contents of other computers. You enter the subject you are seeking and, after a short wait, up pop the results of the search. If your search was successful, each Internet address that holds information concerning the given subjectmatter will be listed on the screen. You just click on the one you think is the most relevant, and it takes you there. It is that simple. Alternatively, a browser will accept an Internet address entered by you. So if you know the address of the service you want, rather than having to search for it, you just type it in and within seconds you are there.

CompuServe

CompuServe is probably the biggest international online service in the world. With its hundreds of thousands of subscribers on an increasingly interconnected planet, being the biggest has its advantages: like the telephone system, people connect to a network because everyone else is there. The system offers conferencing and messaging services, which means it provides discussions and email, and these cover a wide range of topics, some of the most useful of which are news, sport and travel information—you can check airline schedules using CompuServe. CompuServe is also the preferred medium for most computer companies to disseminate information about their products and upgrade (or 'bug-fix') files—useful if you suspect bugs in your system. Although most of the information is US-specific, CompuServe is moving towards a more international model.

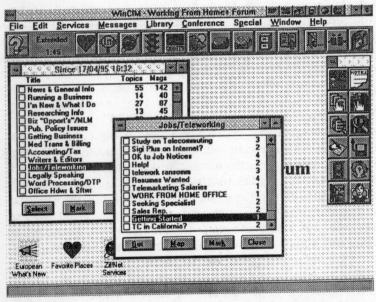

CompuServe is one of the most powerful resources available to the home business. Its large number of 'conference forums' enables users with common interests to participate in discussions.
Illustrated here is the Working from Home forum, where small-business owners and home-workers around the world 'meet' to exchange information, experiences and work opportunities.

It also brings Internet connections, and the software to access the Internet through CompuServe along with instructions on how to use it are on the system; you just type GO INTERNET and it's all there. So with a single subscription to a single service, you can have a link to all CompuServe's subscribers, as well as to anyone with an Internet address. Access to Internet newsgroups (known as Usenet) is also available.

Most of the UK has local call access to CompuServe, or you can get at it via your Internet service provider using telnet: the Internet address is compuserve.com. Subscribing to CompuServe is simple. You call the free 0800 289458 number and they will issue an ID number and tell you what to do next. Basic services cost a few dollars a month (all CompuServe's charges are in US dollars, which are then translated into UK sterling via your credit card).

For more on the Web and CompuServe, including their potential as marketing tools, turn to Chapter 7.

Cix

The Compulink Information Exchange (Cix), the UK's biggest online service, is located in Surbiton, Surrey, and so far it has only London nodes, which makes dialling outside the London area a more expensive business. On the plus side, it is a UK service, which means that unlike CompuServe, the discussions, information and files come from UK sources. For instance, a discussion about the price of a software upgrade, information about the efficiency of a computer company's telephone support, or how to get a network running and where to obtain the various pieces will be relevant in this country.

The main uses you will find for Cix are file downloads and information to help you make the most of the PC. Based around discussion conferences, the information will allow you to find out why this PC graphics card does not work properly with that particular type of hard disk. The problem with it is that much of this information is buried deep in conference discussions and is hard to find; the tools for searching for information in a Cix conference are not as sophisticated as they could be. Files germane to the conference topic are available in most conferences, depending on how the area has been set up, and these are usually fairly well annotated, so you can tell what each set of files is for. Cix also offers faxing facilities, plus mail services that link not just to others on Cix but to anywhere on the Internet.

Using Cix is made much easier (and cheaper) by the development of the offline reader, which we shall cover in more detail in the section on software, below, but essentially it is software that saves you time and money by allowing you to read messages while you are disconnected from the service. Getting onto Cix for the first time involves dialling in using one of three numbers—0181 399 5252 is probably the best to start with—and following instructions; you type 'new' at the login prompt and take it from there. You can access Cix through the Internet too, using telnet (as with CompuServe; the Internet address is cix.compulink.co.uk). There is a minimum cost of a few pounds per month, depending on usage, plus a joining fee.

You will find if you log onto systems like Cix and CompuServe that the biggest problem is winnowing the wheat from the chaff. While Cix's conferences are 'moderated' (there are one or more moderators for each conference whose job is to keep discussions relevant to the subjectmatter for which the conference and sub-topic were set up), the quality of that moderation varies enormously. For instance, some conferences have a sub-topic called 'chatter', which will be very lightly moderated, while users of one called 'networks' may be castigated publicly for straying too far off the beaten track. But online people tend to be very helpful, and if you have a problem they will help you faster and more cheaply than the official technical support, and they will tell you about little wrinkles which the vendors will not. There is, however, an unspoken pact, that you give as much as you take: if you have discovered a new way of making things work, or have found a new source of information, or can help someone else who asks for it, you are honour-bound to tell people about it. It is a community thing.

FIRST PRINCIPLES: GETTING ONLINE

So what kind of hardware and software do you need to get online? There is just one underlying technology that allows you to conduct your business and personal affairs remotely—in other words, from home rather than from your employer's office. It is over 100 years old, and you already know it intimately and use it regularly: the telephone. Add to this any PC that is less than four years old, and a modem. And then you will need communications software—Windows comes with a basic terminal which is perfectly adequate for most purposes, but after a time you will start feeling the need for greater sophistication and more features. For instance, Windows terminal uses Xmodem, a method of transferring files that is very slow and which, if interrupted for any reason, does not allow you to carry on where you left off. Instead you have to transfer the whole file all over again. Zmodem, on the other hand, suffers neither restriction.

Once you are online you will find a wealth of communications programs out there—after all, the one thing that everyone online has in common is the fact that they are there, and that they all need communications programs. After a while you will have a better feel for what your needs are, and be able to ask questions about the best place to find what you are looking for—and most of the computer techies online are more than happy to show you how to find it.

More about modems

Modems were introduced in Chapter 2, but the true online afficionado may wish to know more. If you have ever heard a modem, you might think that the noises it generates are nothing like a voice, but those squeals and whistles fall within the frequency range of the human voice, which the phone system is built to handle. Using a range of clever techniques including compression and multi-level encoding (using a multi-layered barrage of tones to represent a bit, which is the smallest particle of data that the computer understands), a modern modem can squeeze up to 28,800 bits every second down the phone line. If one 650-word page of A4 text is 4,000 characters and each character consists of one byte (eight bits), that makes almost a page which can be sent every second. When PCs first appeared, the average modem transmitted at one-thousandth that speed.

Buying and using a modem

Modems cost relatively little. For less than £100 you can buy one that transmits at 14,400 bits per second, half the top speed mentioned above, but that should make little difference unless you intend to transmit data such as graphical images, which generally consist of huge quantities of data. A picture may well be worth a thousand words, but when it comes to using computers, they take much more space, and then some. Try this: pull up some text in a word processor under Windows. If you converted a digital snapshot of that image on the screen into a file on the hard disk, it could be anything from ten to 100 times bigger than a file containing just the text it is displaying. While there are ways, such as compression, of reducing the size of a file containing a graphical image, you would do well to consider buying the fastest modem you can afford if your work involves or is likely to involve sending and receiving a lot of images. If you are planning to use the World-Wide Web area of the Internet to any extent, for instance, you will be downloading images—quite a lot of them.

Modems are categorised mainly on the basis of their speed, and each speed is allocated a V number by the international committee (the ITU) which sets standards in this area of technology. The standard protocol used by fast modems transmitting at 28,800 bits per second is known as V34, while those working at half the speed use V32bis. Note that the modems at both ends of a connection have to use the same protocol (think of it as a common language between a pair of international delegates), so you cannot connect a V32bis modem to a V34 modem and expect it to work at the highest speed that either of them (in this case the V34 product) is capable of. What they will do, however, is negotiate the highest common speed that each understands.

If they are both fully compatible with the standards (and most are these days), then in this instance you should expect a V32bis-style connection of 14,400 bits per second; in other words, the V34 modem will run at lower speeds than its maximum.

There's just one more issue concerning hardware before we look at the software you will need, and that is the link between the modem and the computer, and between the modem and the phone line.

Cabling

In the case of the former, if it is not supplied with the computer or modem, the cable you need will be known by various names. You may find it under its vernacular title of serial or modem cable, or by its more technically correct RS-232 cable, and its job is to link the modem and your computer's serial port. Either way, the important thing is to look at the back of your computer and check what type of serial port yours is, for you will be using it to access the online world.

There are usually two types of serial or COM port, as it may be labelled, and there may be two ports. Of the two types, the 9-pin is smaller than the 25-pin variety, as you would expect, but for our purposes they are functionally identical. Which of the two your PC's manufacturer has fitted will depend largely on cost and the size of the case into which the system fits. The 9-pin type is the same size as the connector used to convey VGA signals from the computer to your monitor, while the other is considerably wider. There are also two types of each size of connector, a male which has pins that fit into corresponding sockets on the female type. You will need a male connector (with pins) at the modem end, and a female (without pins) at the computer end.

Having verified how many pins your chosen COM socket has, and using the information above, you can confidently go out and buy a serial cable for a modem. If you have two serial or COM ports, it may simplify matters if you use COM1 rather than COM2, as most communications software will assume you want to use that one first. You can of course always change this later.

Linking the modem and phone line is relatively simple, so long as you have a phone socket; if you have one of the older, directly wired types of phone, you will need to change it. The phone line looks (and in fact is) just like the cable used to connect your standard phone to the public service telephone network (PSTN) and, as far as the PSTN is concerned, it neither knows nor cares whether you are putting modem noises or voice noises down the phone line. In other words, there is no extra cost associated with a data call, as opposed to a voice call.

If you decide you want a portable computer because you are likely to use it abroad, the picture changes dramatically and you will have to look for a cable which fits the phone sockets of the country you are visiting. Unfortunately there is no standardisation in this area at all, even down to the order in which the lines inside the phone cable are used. Your first port of call for support in this case should be either the PC or the modem manufacturer, or take a look on one of the online conferencing services: this problem is endemic, and there are several solutions which people online will have come up with.

One final issue associated with modems is official approval. Before a modem maker can sell a modem to the public, it must be approved for connection to the PSTN. The original aim of this was to protect the system and its engineers from unpleasant surprises from wayward signals and voltages, and most responsible modem manufacturers do comply with the approvals process. This then allows them to put a green 'approved' sticker on the box, without which its sale is legal but its actual use on the PSTN is not. The approvals procedure used to be much longer and more expensive for the vendor than it is now, but it still adds considerably to the cost of modem development, so you may find unapproved modems at cheaper prices. Don't buy one. While the lower cost may be tempting and likelihood of discovery remote, you do not know whether it is in fact safe to connect to the PSTN; also, the last thing you want if you are running your own business is a legal hassle over a modem.

SOFTWARE—THE BASICS

Hardware is only a part of the equation. To get online you need communications software, which we touched on in Chapter 2. What this does is provide a window onto a remote computer to make it appear as if, to all intents and purposes, you are sitting in front of the remote machine. So instead of getting the information you see on the screen from the hard disk inside the box on your desk, it uses the serial or COM port and the modem. What kind of software you need depends broadly on what you want to access, although the minimum to get you connected is already supplied with Windows.

If you want to access the Internet, then you have two options. Either you join a service such as Cix or Compu-Serve, find a relevant conference and grab from there the files that allow you to get connected, or, much more simply, you take a look at one of the large and growing number of Internet access kits available. Check out the magazines and advertisements, and pick one with a local exchange number. The kit will usually include the software you need— TCP/IP networking software (already supplied free with Windows 95), plus a WWW browser. Most likely this will be Netscape, which is by far the most popular. Be sure to get hold of a kit that includes free airtime with a POP—you will often get the first few hours of connect time free—and which includes full instructions for installing the software, and advice on what to do during those first few hours online.

Access to the Internet is usually via a third party known as a point of presence or POP. The POP is a company with leased lines that connect its computers to the Internet. You dial into one of the POP's modems, and the link is made. After the usual logging on process—you enter your name and password—your WWW browser takes over, and you are surfing. In return, there is a subscription charge which pays for the upkeep of the POP company's computers, its rental of the leased lines, and provides some profit. You will have to pay your own phone bills too, of course, but if you only log on during off-peak hours and the POP is local (they are springing up all over the country so there should be one contactable for a local call charge) the cost is fairly low.

Basic communications

If the Internet does not figure in your plans, a simple communications package may be all you need. In that case, the first piece of communications software you have probably come across is Windows Terminal, or if you are using Windows 95, HyperTerminal. Terminal does a reasonable if very basic job. It does not, however, provide access to the fastest methods of transferring files online, nor does it give you the ability to save a session to a file on disk; this can be incredibly useful if you want to go back over messages you looked at while online, because you should not have to make another phone call to look at information you have already paid to view: a good cost-cutting principle to observe is to download information once only.

Windows 95's HyperTerminal is a big improvement, and fills in the gaps in Terminal's feature list. There is no reason why you should not carry on using just HyperTerminal if you only access a limited number of services—which is the case with most people.

If you are still using the old DOS/Windows combination, then you might consider using a DOS-only communications program. The advantage is that there are few good Windows communications programs, and also that communications can take a lot of processing power, depending on what kind of COM port your PC manufacturer has provided (see p. 71). Windows also takes a good deal of processing power, so your communications program can end up struggling; if you have got a slow machine and are running Windows versions 3.1 or 3.11, leave Windows and use DOS for your communications work.

The best DOS comms package is Odyssey 2.0. It is simple to use, yet provides a wide range of powerful features, with the most-used ones easily accessible. Like most advanced communications packages, it has a scripting language, which means that if you go online a lot and use a lot of services, it will automate the process for you. You really do not want to get into writing your own scripts unless you are interested in programming, but the program comes with ready-made scripts that are easily adapted—or alternatively and much better, you can tell the program to record what you do and replay it later.

What this means is that the package can pick up the phone, log on, collect your mail, read through the conferences you are interested in, log off again, and put the phone down, all without your intervention. After you are logged off and the phone is back on the hook, you can read through the messages in the conferences of which you are a member, simply by reading through a file on the hard disk, because Odyssey will have captured the text that was sent by the remote system and saved it. But this method has several drawbacks, not least of which is that it does not allow you easily to reply to messages. However, there are better ways of going about such tasks using an offline reader application, which we looked at in the section on Cix, above. You do not have to use the package that way, of course; like any other communications program, you can simply work interactively while you are online, but that does tend to lead to higher phone bills.

Under Windows, Odyssey for Windows 2.0 is hard to beat too, and offers many of the same advantages but using a Windows look and feel. Both programs suffer from the same disadvantage, however. They present you with the raw slabs of text that issue from the remote computer. All online services look different from each other and they often require detailed knowledge of a set of typed-in commands that drive the service and give you access to the information you want. It is less than satisfactory, so to make these remote services easier for the ordinary person to use, the so-called offline and online readers have been developed.

Each such package is normally dedicated for use with a specific service. Running under Windows, what such programs do is take the raw text from the remote computer and display it in a graphical manner that makes it easy to navigate. So instead of typing a command to move to the next message or to see a list of files that are available for retrieval, you just point and click with the Windows mouse pointer. The difference is that online readers do it while you are still connected and paying charges, while offline readers do it more cheaply, at your leisure.

The most prominent example of an offline reader is Ameol, Cix's official offline interface. Like the other examples of this kind of software, Ameol works by automating the entire process of logging on, and then reproduces the conferences that you normally use on your hard disk. In effect, it gives you a local copy of the areas of Cix that you normally access. You can then browse through the various messages and file lists at your leisure without the pressure of knowing that every second is costing you money in phone charges. Any messages that you post in response to those you have read while offline are transmitted (uploaded) the next time you instruct the software to log on. You can download the latest version of Ameol from the Ameol conference.

Best known of the online readers is WinCim, which works with CompuServe. It is available across a wide range of bulletin boards, and of course on CompuServe itself. It sits between you and CompuServe, and allows you to drive the service using Windows. So to retrieve messages in a particular conference (or forum, as they are called on CompuServe), you type in the name of the forum (or pick it from a list that the program will build up and save for you as you use the service) and you are presented with a list of headings and the number of messages in each heading. The headings are normally the sub-topics set up by the forum's moderators—called sysops on CompuServe, which is computer-speak for SYStem OPerator and is pronounced 'sissop'.

Hype surrounding the Internet makes it appear more alien than it truly is: in fact it is people interacting, and while the pioneers tended to be those with a special interest in computers, this is no longer so; it is becoming more cosmopolitan by the day. Online services Cix and CompuServe between them will probably meet most of your needs—if not, they provide useful gateways both for the Internet and as mediums for finding out more about specialised services your business may need.

And while the hardware is getting cheaper, it is also getting easier to use. The barriers are coming down, and the prospect of getting hooked up is more appealing, from both a personal and a business point of view. The earlier you do it, the greater the advantage you will accrue.

5 Strategies for Working From Home

Acquiring, setting up and using computer technology is barely the beginning of your career at home. Assuming you have got the business basics in place, your biggest challenge is now the day-to-day management of your workload, your time and the other myriad issues involved in working at home. The plus points are easy to spot, and some of them are probably the reason why you are working at home in the first place. Freedom, flexibility, greater control over your life and the opportunity to forget commuting for ever surely rank highly among the priorities of anyone who has ever travelled to work for a large corporation every day. But it is as well to be aware of the problems you are likely to face before they arise, some of which you can foresee and others which may be totally unexpected. You may think that more time with your family is a big bonus, but it may turn out that you—or your family—find that the reality does not live up to the ideal. You might relish the prospect of sending out your own invoices, but don't forget the hidden costs on which you are going to have to spend your earnings: heating, lighting and telephones, which formerly an employer would have absorbed.

THE ERGONOMIC OFFICE

Before you get engrossed in the details of your computer, the software and whatever tasks you have undertaken, you need to be sure that you are fit and healthy. For the home-worker, this means far more than taking your vitamins and switching to skimmed milk: in an office where *you* are controlling your working hours, you need to pay close attention to the basic ergonomics of your furniture, office layout and working habits. The weak points of the home-based teleworker are the wrists and hands, which can develop repetitive strain injury; the eyes, which can become sore and red, causing irritation and headache; and the neck and shoulder muscles, which easily tense up, creating fatigue, tension and pain. Avoid these problems (which can become crippling if neglected) by preparing your environment and equipment with these issues in mind; but above all, develop and maintain good working habits. For a more detailed account of these health problems and how to prevent them, see *The Computer User's Health Handbook*, by Joanna Bawa.

Space

Begin by identifying your office space. Wherever possible, a separate room with no other function is preferable to a corner of the living room, or the dining room when it is not being a dining room. Indeed, many employers (not unreasonably) stipulate that telecommuting staff must have a suitable room in which to work when they are working for the company. You will also find that a separate room makes it easier for you to demarcate your work and your personal life. Physical actions such as locking the office door at the weekend or in the evenings can have a profound psychological effect on your desire to work during these hours, and you are less likely to develop bad habits such as watching television or chatting with passing family members while you work (you're also less likely to be shamed into clearing the washing up, vacuuming the carpet or dusting the stereo). A lack of private space for your office could finish off your teleworking career before it really gets going.

Environment

For your own health and sanity, you need a room that is comfortable, warm and well lit. If it has a window, so much

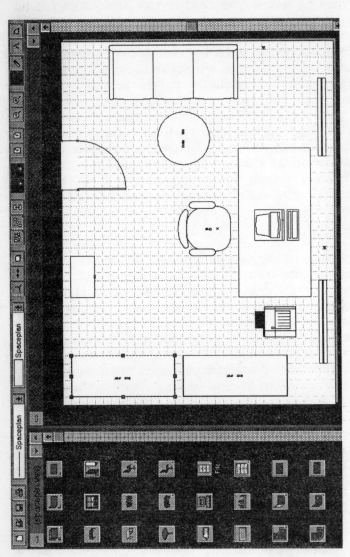

Planning and arranging your work space is a prerequisite for the successful SOHO worker. Planning and diagramming software such as Visio (shown here) makes spatial and charting tasks more manageable.

the better; if not, you will need a ceiling light and an adjustable desk lamp to provide both general and focused light. Heating is obviously important and can become expensive, so the more efficient the system you have, the better. Otherwise, be sure to build heating bills into your charges if you are working alone, and negotiate a deal well in advance with your employer if you are telecommuting.

Furniture

A kitchen table as a desk might seem like a fine idea, but it is well worth investing in proper office furniture for your home office. This way it is far easier to pick a desk and chair that work well together, conform to established ergonomic standards (such as BS5940) and will not suddenly be needed if you have guests for dinner. They also help make you feel you are really at work rather than messing around at home, and if there are drawers built in beneath, they can provide additional storage space for papers and stationery. A comfortable office chair with adjustable back support, arm rests and height control is not a luxury, and a five-point swivel chair can be more easily moved if you need the room for something else; office desks generally have enough room beneath them to conceal printer, system unit and monitor if need be.

Accessories

There is a wide range of so-called 'ergonomic' accessories available, intended to make your working life easier and more comfortable, but they will have little effect unless they are bought as part of an overall plan. Even the best anti-glare screen, for example, will provide little benefit if your office layout is such that you cannot avoid direct light falling on your monitor. Sensible strategies include restricting your purchases to those items that will make a noticeable difference to your comfort, which will in turn depend on your working practices. Intensive keyboard users (writers, transcribers and some programmers) can justify an ergonomic keyboard with wrist rest; graphic artists and designers may derive more benefit from a high resolution monitor or an ergonomic mouse. Physical characteristics such as height or existing back problems may make a footrest or more expensive chair a worthwhile purchase.

Healthy working habits

None of the above will help you a great deal if you persist in working every second God sends without giving your poor frail body even the shortest break. By far the simplest, cheapest and most effective ergonomics is the practice of rest breaks—taking short but regular breaks, right away from the computer and even the office. A good rule of thumb is to take short breaks, perhaps no more than thirty seconds or so, every five to ten minutes; then take a longer, ten-minute break, at the end of each hour. Try to include a more substantial break, an hour at least, at a point that divides your working day in two. During the short breaks (micropauses), try a simple stretching exercise, look away from the screen and out of the window, or just stand up and sit down again. Longer breaks justify a brief stroll around the house or garden, another cup of coffee or a period of social telephoning. In your main break, get right away from the working environment. For those who simply forget to stop, there are software products around that will record your working time (or typing rate) and remind you when to take a break, and for how long.

WORKING AT HOME: PROBLEMS AND SOLUTIONS

Working at home is fraught with difficulties, some of which are trivial, some more serious. Some will be apparent even before you set up your home office; others may not emerge until you are well into your home-working career. Like all such problems, the trick is to pre-empt them and deal with them before they become a major worry.

Problem: perceived low status

In the normal office environment, the way you are perceived by colleagues, managers and clients depends on your status, and your status depends on their perceptions and behaviour. Maintaining status—and the behaviours it generates, such as respect, phone calls, requests for involvement—from a home office is much more difficult for a variety of reasons.

Working alone without a network of colleagues means you have to create your own status and ensure that clients and potential clients perceive you as a substantial and worthwhile contact. You are largely invisible to begin with, so the traditional trappings of status (car, corner office, leather swivel chair) become meaningless, but there are other, more subtle ways in which home-working can detract from your status in the working world. Despite many steps forward in perceptions of work and workers, there is still an ingrained assumption that going out to work is a 'masculine' activity, while staying at home is 'feminine'. For everyone, therefore, announcing that you work at home can sometimes be construed as implying you are not serious, your heart is not in it, you don't have the resources of a large office behind you.

The status of home-workers can also be a gender issue: home-working retains connotations of traditionally feminine employment: housework, nurturing and child-care. This should not matter, but to be perceived as 'serious' or 'professional' in a work context usually implies an external work location, and preferably a powerful position commanding a high salary. Women, therefore, have a different set of status issues to contend with when working at home. Without the support of an external employer, there is a risk that working from home via technology will return women to the low-status role of being 'just' a housewife in a way that cannot affect men. In some cases the perception may even hold true: men are less likely to notice (far less assume responsibility for) the day-to-day functioning of a household, and may find it easier to block out extraneous domestic interruptions—the pile of dirty washing, the blocked sink or the lack of anything in the fridge for dinner. For women, this may be compounded by externally employed husbands who not only carry on expecting normal domestic routines to continue, but believe that a home-based wife can accommodate shopping, cleaning, cooking and child-care with far greater ease than before.

Solution: how to be taken seriously

Get taken seriously by presenting yourself as someone serious. To begin with, there is no need to admit, straight away, that you work at home. When trying to impress a potential new client, do what any company does: focus on what you do and how well you do it, and back up your claims with a portfolio of existing work for prestigious clients. Dress as you would to meet such a client—suit, briefcase and smart haircut—and where possible arrange meetings on clients' premises. If that is inconvenient, book an office in a hotel for the afternoon. Invest in your image and start out with at least a smart business card and headed notepaper—if at all possible, include an email address on a business card. Once you have built up trust and met your professional obligations consistently, you might want to explain your arrangements—or you might not. Whatever you decide, downplay the fact that you work at home. It is not relevant to the quality of your work and it is not a big deal for you, so there is no reason why it should matter to a client.

Problem: knowing when to start—and stop

The clean slate of a whole day ahead of you may seem exhilarating, but it can also be daunting. Without the normal routines of an office day it can be difficult to 'get down to it' when necessary, and the temptations and distractions are many and varied. If work is booming you can run into difficulties with priorities, meeting commitments and setting reasonable deadlines. It is all too easy to end up working round the clock without a break, only to burn out halfway through an important project or fall prey to a bout of panic. If time is slack, the problems are monotony, boredom, lowered self-esteem and slipping morale. In either case, you need to beware of blurring the boundaries between work and personal time: however much you enjoy your work, it must not be allowed to impinge on leisure, relaxation and social activities; however compelling that soap opera, it does not have to be watched during your mid-afternoon work session—record it.

Solution: structuring time

Totally open-ended time is scary. Shrink and slice it to manageable proportions by maintaining a regular work schedule, especially the beginning and ending of the working day. At first, follow typical office patterns to maintain a sense of rhythm: a couple of hours' intensive work in the morning when you are fresh; short breaks when you need them; a lunch break and steadily paced work in the afternoon. Once you establish a pattern, it will help you stay focused. It is also an opportunity for family and friends to learn when you will and will not be available and to stick to those times, leaving you free to concentrate on both work and play.

As you develop a rhythm of your own, you may find that you would prefer to devote mornings to intensive working and afternoons to less pressured telephoning or administration; or perhaps you would rather get up late, ease yourself gently into the office and achieve fever-pitch work intensity in the evenings or wee small hours. Experiment to find what works best for you. Previous office patterns may have convinced you that no good work gets done after 3.00 pm, which may be true if you started at 8.00 am, but not if you started at 11.00. Your evenings may once have been sacred socialising time but now serve better as creative work sessions. Work at different times to find out when you can concentrate and when you just feel tired, but bear in mind that whilst it is a good idea to establish a rhythm it is also important to build in flexibility—you may need to work intensively in the mornings *and* evenings on some occasions.

The 'time-wasters' of office life—chatting, attending meetings, writing and reading memos, attending more meetings—do not apply to the home-worker, but there are plenty of substitutes to lure you away from your desk. Use these techniques to recognise and avoid them: each time you begin a routine domestic task, switch on the television or feel an urge to catch up with the weeding, ask yourself:

- Do I need to do this?
- Do I need to do it *now*?
- Will anything suffer if I don't do this now, or at all?
- Which will suffer most—my domestic harmony or my living?
- Why am I *really* doing this—is it because it needs to be done or because I want to avoid doing something else?

If you are simply using the task as a means of avoiding work, you need some motivational tips (see below).

Starting work
Create definite beginnings and endings to your working day within which you can afford to be flexible, but focused and hard-working. Start by developing rituals to get yourself going on the working day until you become comfortable with them as signals that it is time to get down to it. Pick something easy or enjoyable—checking for new mail (paper or electronic); updating your address file with new leads; phoning to confirm the next meeting—even preparing a pot of coffee. Once this is completed, you will be settled into a calmer, more concentrated frame of mind. You can also start work when you hear the closing music of a morning news show, watch children leave for school or a spouse for work, or after exercise. Structure the next few hours by deciding what, at the end of the day, you intend to have accomplished and organise those things into a priority list. Make sure you are aware of the implications if you miss a deadline or fail to meet your targets—even if the cost is only going to be a sense of personal failure. The process can be a constructive

and positive one if you choose targets that are realistic and manageable and which can be achieved in the time available. Write them down if it helps to make them more definite.

Stopping work

At the other end of the spectrum (or the day!) is the difficulty of knowing when to stop. Unlike your office colleagues, there is no set moment at which you can revert to your 'home persona' or remove your suit. When you are just yards from your office, it takes extra strength and discipline to switch off the computer, turn on the answerphone and relax back into family life, and sometimes extra techniques are needed. Muffle enticing sounds (the fax machine or telephone) by turning down speakers or placing them at the far corner of your office; turn off heaters so that the room becomes less comfortable after hours; install an elaborate blind or heavy curtains which need time to open; or simply lock the door. Workaholism can be a serious threat to your work and family life, and it is important to establish patterns that will discourage clients or colleagues from contacting you 'after hours'. If you intend to work in the evenings (rather than, say, mornings) make sure this is clear (to family as well as clients) and keep your private hours private.

Finally, stop measuring your performance in terms of time-at-the-desk, and don't compare your work patterns with those of your office-bound colleagues. It is hard to judge how much work you are doing out of the office, but most experienced telecommuters will tell you that they get more done at home than in the office. The eight-hour working day has always been a myth: few, if any, people put in this much time at the office once you subtract lunch, breaks, useless meetings and interruptions, so your five-hour stint may well be something to be proud of. Pace yourself by projects undertaken and goals met by deadline, where deadlines are set after negotiation between you and your client. And since a lot of people expect home-workers to spend time messing around, make sure you build some messing-around time in to suit them.

Problem: knowing what to do first

You will probably start your home-working career full of enthusiasm and eager to get on with it. The chances are that the initial euphoria will not last and you will need to develop a smoother, more sustainable pattern, dealing with tasks as they arise in a planned sequence, rather than tackling everything at once. There is also a danger that in your anxiety to impress clients or colleagues (or yourself) you might take on work that does not enhance your experience, your reputation or your fulfilment. Learning to allocate priorities and choose work that allows you to move in a particular direction is a skill that relies heavily on your having a clear idea of exactly what it is you want to achieve, at a very high level. Do you want to be amazingly rich? A better parent? Your own boss? A recognised expert? A secure player in a niche market? Knowing your real goal and understanding your true motivation are essential to developing a working style that's manageable, successful—and makes you happy.

Solution: setting and meeting goals

Start by contemplating why you have become more involved in your home computer and what it is you want to be remembered for. If it does not spring to mind immediately, dredge up old dreams and wild ambitions and try to identify a common theme; mould it into something which can be articulated clearly and simply and remember it as the ultimate goal of your business.

Once you have got your ultimate goal sorted out, it becomes easier to define sub-goals and work towards them more realistically. Distinguish between goals and priorities —priorities are those elements of your life and career which are important; goals support these priorities. For example, your personal priority may be to become fitter and slimmer; your goal would then be to attend an aerobics class twice a week, starting today. Your professional priority may be to get your name on the lips of everyone who is influential in your field; your goal could be to send a press release to these people once a month, with sub-goals of identifying precisely who these people are and creating a contact database within a month of starting work. Goals are precise and well-planned statements, containing both specific objectives ('to get a regular commission from the arts page of a national newspaper') and target dates ('by the end of 1995'). Three to five major goals can generally encapsulate your broadest ambitions—more than that means you are trying to achieve too much or have not thought carefully enough about what you want.

Problem: getting on with it

Anyone who has ever had to take an examination will remember that period of revision: stuck at home, desperately trying to concentrate on something deeply boring whilst resisting the sudden appeal of television, rearranging the furniture or even doing the ironing. The discipline of home-working can seem similarly difficult, and even the most diligent worker can become distracted and find it harder and harder to stay motivated, even when there is a pressing need to complete tasks.

Solution: staying motivated

What motivates someone is very personal and can vary widely between different people. If you are working at home, however, there is a good chance that you are motivated by the work you are doing and the satisfaction you gain from running your own life. The first thing, therefore, when you find yourself gazing listlessly out of the window, is to ask yourself how much you enjoy what you are doing and whether you are really happy with your home-based working life. If you are bored, stuck in a rut or can no longer see the point, you may need to rethink your overall objectives and the way you go about achieving them. If you find your work intrinsically interesting and challenging, sooner or later you will want to get on with it.

Do something different

Remember that everyone needs variety, and a break now
and again. If fatigue is becoming a problem, simply do
something different—the more different from your work,
the better. Get away from the office (or your working
environment), do the ironing, go shopping, drive around
the area. To avoid getting too absorbed in your new
activity, set a time limit on yourself or, if that is too hard,
trick yourself into getting back in time—leave something
in the oven, hang washing out when it looks like rain, ask a
client to call you at a certain time. If the mood continues
when you are back in the office, start on those tedious,
low-priority but must-be-done chores—tidying your in-
tray, filing, paying the bills, sorting your journals into
chronological order, cleaning those sticky coffee mug
stains from your desk. The routine will soothe your
agitation without putting a heavy load on your thinking
capabilities, and when you have finished you will feel as if
you have accomplished a great deal. Trivial and easily
avoided tasks can prey on your conscience without your
realising it; by attending to them, you clear space in your
mind—and on your desk.

Set yourself deadlines

Be brutal and tell yourself to get it done by the end of the
day. A tight deadline helps you focus—make it tighter than
you would if delegating the same task to a colleague and
gain extra achievement points by meeting it. It does not
matter if you don't have a real deadline; set one anyway and
watch achievements emerging. You will probably find that
other tasks get done more efficiently as well. If the task is
simply too big to be done within a manageable time frame,
don't be afraid to take time out of your schedule—a whole
day if necessary—to plan. Break the task down into smaller,
more manageable sub-tasks and allocate shorter periods to
each of them. Whilst each little nibble at a large project
might seem insignificant, the amount you will achieve as
they add up can be enormous.

Extortion and bribery
Cajole yourself into working with threats and rewards. In slack moments, remind yourself that time away from your home office is time when you *are not* earning money, then pin the bills up around you to remind yourself what you owe to others. Then, once you are frightened into action, add a few bribes. Reward yourself for completing difficult tasks, on time. It could be something trivial, like reading the next chapter of that gripping novel, or something substantial, like booking a night away in a favourite bed-and-breakfast. Fit the reward to the task: when you finish a first draft, go for a walk; when you complete a final version, take someone you love (or just like) out for dinner; when you cash the cheque, take off for the weekend. Choose rewards that make you happy—you may need a new printer cartridge more urgently, but it probably won't motivate you as much as a bottle of champagne.

Simulate life at the office
What would colleagues say if you downed tools and started painting the window frames or sorting through the cutlery drawer? If domestic distractions are clamouring for your attention, remind yourself that in a real office you wouldn't even be aware of them, let alone worrying whether they got done or not. Switch off the music, shut the door and pretend you are in a real office. When interruptions occur, ask yourself how you would handle them if you worked away from home. Then handle them that way.

Look after yourself
Only the most naive home-worker still believes that sitting in front of a computer means good work is getting done. You need regular breaks during the working day and plenty of rest afterwards to stay fresh and creative: increase your productivity by taking a 20-minute break every 90 minutes or so. Everyone has their own rhythm—when they are alert, when they are sleepy—and you should learn and pay attention to yours. This can be more complex than simply knowing whether you are a 'lark' (early riser and sleeper) or an

'owl' (get up and retire late), since rhythms vary during the day, too. Most of us are familiar with the 'post-lunch dip', the sleepiness that sets in around 2.30 pm, especially if you have had a good lunch. Reduce its effects and even out mood swings by sticking to high-protein, low-fat lunches and avoiding alcohol; stay clear-headed by swapping sugary snacks for dried fruit, wholegrain biscuit bars or nuts.

Good nutrition at all times is essential, and plenty of water alongside the coffee will keep you alert and reduce headaches. Don't skip breakfast, either for time or for diet reasons—you need a morning meal to kick-start your metabolism into action after sleeping. Without it, you will stay ticking over at low levels for far longer: blood sugar remains low, causing fatigue early in the day, and your body will burn fewer calories later on.

If at all possible, don't work when you are not well—no one is there to appreciate your noble stand, and you will delay your recovery. If you absolutely must get the job done, take it as gently as possible and try to warn your client if sickness might mean a delay. Most people will understand that this happens and will extend deadlines; if not, take extra rest once the work is completed.

Problem: loneliness and isolation

When they say, 'You're on your own now', it has a metaphorical ring, but for the home-based worker it can be all too true. In fact, for many people, isolation is the toughest part of working alone. If you are used to having colleagues around to share ideas, chat, gossip and brainstorm, the raw reality of a small work-space and your own soul can be a tremendous shock. The problem is not so much the obvious one—that nobody else is physically working in the same office as you—it is more to do with the fact that nobody else is aware of the work you are doing or is concerned with how you are getting on. It is dangerously easy to start questioning the entire meaning and purpose of your chosen path when there's no one to reinforce and reward your efforts, and the uncomfortable conviction that everyone's having a better time than you becomes all too familiar. The work can become less rewarding too: away from the office environment, you miss out on the chance to see how your own work fits in with other people's and it is less likely that you will get to see the finished result or claim your share of the credit and celebrations.

Tackling these feelings isn't easy, nor should you expect any measures you take to be totally effective. One of your strongest defences against loneliness is an awareness of how common it is and how low it can bring you—even when it is no more or less than anyone else in your position has experienced. Once you are prepared for this, loneliness becomes much easier to recognise and deal with.

Solution: managing social and personal contact time

Ward off feelings of loneliness and isolation by preparing for the event before it happens. Turn your social life into another aspect of your business and develop contact habits which become a regular part of your routine. As part of your start-up ritual, perhaps, discipline yourself to make one social call a day. It does not have to be a different person each time, but obviously you should not be concentrating your efforts on one unsuspecting individual. Maybe you can work through your address book once, person by person, identify who has got the time or the interest, and stay in contact with a smaller number of people more or less regularly. The call should not be a big deal, though—a brief chat will help keep you sane and 'visible'; any more may cause resentment amongst busy friends. Try to commit yourself to one social get-together a week—either visit or entertain—and keep it informal. The important thing is to generate a steady and sustainable throughput of friends who will remind you of who you are and why you chose to work at home. It sounds contrived, but you will soon realise how much you depended on the 'natural' and effortless contact that office work afforded. If you work alone you have to make an effort to maintain your social life. Friends won't just bump into you now, you will need to work at it.

Once you have developed the habit of staying in touch, there are other good habits that will not only maintain the old friendships you need, but help you discover and nurture new ones.

Make breakfast or lunch dates with friends and clients
Some social interaction in the middle of the day is a good change of pace. If you are lunching with a former colleague, you will have a chance to talk shop with someone who understands the minutiae of your work. If it is hard to spare two hours in the middle of the day, try to arrange appointments with clients and suppliers to allow for lunch with a friend in their area. Failing that, befriend established clients and make briefing and update meetings an opportunity to develop closer personal ties. Managed carefully, this can strengthen your business relationship too.

Join a midday dance or exercise class
Physical activity helps stimulate creative thinking. It is good for you, breaks up your routine and puts you with other people for part of the day. If the class is at a local community centre or college, take the opportunity to scan nearby noticeboards for information about other local activities and classes. Working at home can be a great chance to become more involved with your local community.

Join local professional associations
Look out for local business groups or specialist hobbyist groups which meet regularly and where you could contribute. Your interest does not have to be directly professional: whilst it might be of more interest for you to join a software users' group or PC enthusiasts' club, there may be surprising benefits in joining a more specialist or academic group. In addition to the social enjoyment of mingling with others, you may also develop some good business leads. Perhaps the group, or an individual member, could benefit from your technical or business skills—the less technical the group's orientation, the greater your chances of a business 'in'.

Start your own home-workers' support group

For the enthusiastic and committed, taking the initiative can be the key to developing new friends and business contacts. If you can invest the time (and a small amount of money) in recruiting potential contacts, the rewards can be immense. Put announcements in a local newspaper, at an office-supply store, copy shop or fax bureau and ask around for news of other home-workers. Once you have had some interest, start off with informal meetings at a local café or other community building (a library or pub, for example) and take it from there. You may need to be the organiser for the first few weeks, but if it works, others can be encouraged to host meetings at their own homes, or drum up support for further events. Once a comfortable 'arrangement' has been established (every alternate Thursday in the Rose and Crown, for example), you can more or less leave members to get on with it.

Problem: being everywhere at once

Meetings can be one of life's biggest time-wasters. Everyone recognises this but still they go on, creating a dilemma for the home-worker. On the one hand, the whole point of your working at home is to eliminate the costly and unproductive process of travelling to and attending meetings, but on the other hand, you need to maintain a physical presence in the minds of your clients or colleagues—and you need to know what is going on. The persistence of meetings is partly explained by the fact that, when they work, they work well. Important information can be distributed effectively to those people who need it, objections can be raised and dealt with straight away and everyone is made aware of their role in relation to other attendees. Meetings also serve an important psychological function by allowing people to believe that they must be doing something right and something valuable, a force which shouldn't be underestimated. Such factors can overcome even poorly managed and unnecessary meetings, to the cost of the remote worker who has travelled in especially.

Luckily, there are constructive alternatives for the home-based worker. Some are simple replacements for meetings, others are more to do with techniques for getting more out of meetings when you are there, or recognising when it is important to attend—and when it is important not to.

Solution: alternatives and enhancements to meetings

Voice mail or answerphones can be appropriate and effective alternatives to meetings. If the information to be conveyed is straightforward and requires no discussion—the clarification of a brief, a contact name or number, an acknowledgement of receipt—there is obviously no need to attend a meeting. Even quite complex information can be conveyed this way, since it is recorded and can be replayed. Email plays an equally important role—so long as the senders appreciate that at home you are not getting the same level of non-verbal communication as they are and won't 'pick up' on what is going on in the same way.

If you need to *organise* a meeting, do your best to make sure there is plenty of quality time involved. Get commitments from relevant people that they will be there and be sure they know why. Be clear about the purpose of the meeting and prepare an agenda in advance. Assume the role of chairperson and encourage participants to move swiftly along through the items.

If you have to *attend* someone else's meeting, try to be there early enough to get acquainted with others. This is still important when you know participants, perhaps more so than when you don't, since it gives you time to catch up on less formal but equally useful small talk. It also helps to ensure that colleagues remember you as an individual with a personality, rather than a business tool with a function to perform. In either case, allow enough time for the meeting, and overestimate rather than underestimate.

When and when not to meet
If all the information you expect to get from a meeting can be sent to you, it may be worth staying away. Consider

whether meetings are informative or routine, and whether or not you can request information in advance. If this is possible, meetings can be reduced in duration and frequency. It is obviously in your interests to keep meeting times to a minimum, but there are occasions when face-to-face meetings make more sense:

- *Personal introduction*. The first time you meet a client or join a team (especially if they know each other and you are the new boy or girl) you really need to meet and size each other up. It is still the best way to form a bond and maintain a strong team.
- *Discussion or negotiation*. You can't have the give-and-take you need over the phone or computer; do it in person.
- *Important messages*. Major disruptions, a client who needs careful handling or just the biggest contract you have ever landed are too important to risk any sort of misunderstanding; be there.
- *Brainstorming*. People will not be able to share ideas and build on each other's thoughts as effectively if they are not together.
- *Shocking or emotional messages*. Your neglected spouse has walked out, your client has gone bust, your computer crashed. Get news of disaster to those who need to know *quickly*, then arrange an emergency meeting to deal with the shock, the questions and the implications.

Problem: children and spouses still need time and attention

If the loneliness doesn't get you, the family will. Working at home *might* mean working alone, but it might equally well mean tucking yourself away into a corner whilst the hubbub of family life goes on around you. People coming and going, shouting and slamming doors, encroaching on your space and disturbing your work possessions, or even just wanting to talk to you, can be a maddening distraction; and it is quite likely that your hours of work will have to be arranged around what is convenient for them rather than you.

On the other hand, you may have undertaken your at-home venture to spend more time with the family, especially young children, and found that it has not worked out quite as you expected. What seemed like your own time has suddenly become the property of anyone who wants an errand run, a child collected from school or a bit of emergency shopping brought home. Children particularly can be demanding at all hours of the night and day—but clients will not wait.

Solution: managing child care and family relationships

That teleworking is the solution to child care problems is a myth. If you are serious about your work, you will need to make suitable child care arrangements so that you will not get called away from important work or meetings at the slightest thing. What you *can* expect is greater flexibility in your ability to make arrangements at previously difficult times (especially during the day); shorter journeys to rescue a sick or home-coming child and slightly greater opportunities for impromptu play sessions. The unexpected, however, and the constancy of routine daily care (for very young children) require more than the few minutes you will have to spare every now and then.

The progress of family relationships in general depends a lot on whether one or both partners are relocating their work into the home. If one partner is at home already, whether working or not, there are different implications again. A sudden dramatic increase in the number of hours that couples spend in each other's company can be a great opportunity to get to know each other again in a slightly different capacity, whereby the relationship is much enriched through shared experience. On the other hand, there is perhaps a greater chance that prolonged intimacy will become stifling and unbearable.

Newly home-based women teleworkers are likely to experience the issues rather differently from their male counterparts. Whilst it is not unreasonable for the partner at home to open the door for the gas meter reader or arrange a time for the plumber to call, it is definitely overstepping the mark to expect them to assume responsibility for the shopping, cleaning and cooking. Many women find it hard to resist the feeling that these are tasks which they should manage, whereas men, who have traditionally played less of a role in household management, might find it easier to concentrate just on their 'real' work. It can also be uncomfortable for non-working women whose husbands have brought their office home after redundancy or retirement: suddenly there is someone else in the house during the previously sacrosanct daytime hours and, whilst they have established comfortable routines, their partners may be floundering with time management, business issues and life changes.

Managing these relationships is not a straightforward matter and will vary from couple to couple and family to family. What is important is to bear in mind that your decision to set up an office at home impacts directly on everyone who shares that home with you, and that they will suffer your teething pains every bit as much as you. Consultation, joint planning and even just chatting about it can bring those involved into the discussion, enabling them to feel that your plans have not been imposed. If they have helped to make the decision and prepare the ground, they will be less likely to feel awkward or resentful later.

6   Telecommuting: Career Changes, Breaks and Restarts

Telecommuting is the practice—not to say the art and science—of working at home whilst employed by an external organisation, for that organisation. In the context of this book the term *telecommuting* is used specifically to imply that an external employer is involved in the equation, unlike, for instance, a *teleworker*, who uses similar technology for similar reasons but is basically working for him- or herself. The terms are commonly interchangeable, but remain separate here since the issues each raises are very different.

Why telecommute? You have a job, in an office, with an employer. You take home a salary at the end of every month. You have to travel from your home to your employer's office and back every day, making you a commuter. If you now remove the tedious and time-consuming travelling period and replace it with a computer at home and a telephone link to your office, you are a telecommuter.

Telecommuting is, on the surface, a very attractive prospect for employees and employers alike. In purely commercial terms, it offers employers the opportunity to reduce overheads—office space and heating—without losing valued skills and experience. For employees, telecommuting means more quality time for friends and family, less stress and improved productivity. Everyone wins.

If telecommuting is such a win-win work option, why aren't more companies doing it? The answer is that, like most corporate and technological issues, it is not as easy to run a successful telecommuting programme as it appears. The unsuspected problems are many and varied and the ingredients for success are not always obvious. To their credit, many UK firms are investigating the possibilities of telecommuting and increasing numbers are beginning to dip their toes in the murky waters of this uncharted area. By 1996 it is predicted that more than two-thirds of UK companies will have at least a proportion of telecommuters.

Who can telecommute?

Profitable job activities that work well at home are discussed in Chapter 1, but not all of these apply to corporations and their employees. Statistically (and intuitively), the employees of computer companies and other high-tech employees are more likely to become telecommuters. This is not just because their work lends itself more directly to home-based working, or because they have easier access to the required technology: more importantly, it is often because their managers have a clearer understanding of what is involved and how it can be of benefit to the employee as well as the organisation.

This level of support and encouragement is perhaps the most important aspect of a telecommuting programme. Jobs that 'travel' well include anything where the main task of the employee is intellectual, creative or administrative—designing, writing, compiling or composing, planning and researching are some of the broad categories of work that adapt readily to the home office. As technology and software adjust and improve, these categories will broaden and increase. But telecommuting is a great deal more than technology: personalities are involved, not simply computers and modems, and as with any kind of work, not everyone is suited to it. A successful telecommuting programme must take account of the people who are participating—their needs and wants, their motives and perceived gains—if it is to work.

TELECOMMUTING AND PERSONALITY

What does telecommuting mean? Freedom or isolation? Control or anarchy? Home comforts or torments? A lot depends on your personality and circumstances, and that means that telecommuting is not for everyone. A large number of people who successfully work from home are better able to rely on their own internal judgements and evaluations in making decisions, and are less reliant on the opinions and judgements of others. Telecommuting is also a positive decision for most who enjoy it: such people see the gains they achieve rather than the hassles they will avoid. These include increased control over their lives, more time with their families and less expenditure on travel, all of which appear to be greater motivators than the avoidance of rush hour traffic jams, office politics and stress.

This ties in with observations that most home-based workers are motivated by challenges, possibilities and new opportunities instead of remaining in a familiar routine with rigid ways of doing things or established procedures. They are also more proactive in their work lives, and prefer to act to make events happen, in marked contrast to people who wait to respond to events and are prone to engaging in analytical work. It is worth bearing in mind that the downside of constant proactivity is that home-based entrepreneurs often make many mistakes before they learn to weigh risks fully and understand the consequences.

According to some researchers, the most important quality of the telecommuter is self-discipline—the ability to force yourself, regularly, to carry out the sort of tasks you would normally rather avoid. These can be psychological preparations for organised work, such as making the bed or washing dishes, through to actual work disciplines— switching on the computer by 9.30 am or doing the bills every Wednesday. Even apparently unnecessary habits, such as wearing a suit and tie, can help you develop a more work-orientated frame of mind. This is important for motivation, especially when there is no one else to tell you that your deadline is in an hour, no clocks are ticking and there is no work-orientated atmosphere to encourage you. It almost goes without saying that telecommuters need to be well organised, good at time management, flexible, trustworthy and self-confident. It is also commonly assumed that introverts, preferring their own company and a quiet life, will make good telecommuters, but this is not necessarily true. Because telecommuting requires continued interaction with an office, successful participants need to be good team workers and communicators: introverts who prefer to work alone can be a problem to monitor and are less likely to volunteer information about their progress or difficulties.

Psychologists who assess people for temperamental suitability use questionnaires to identify those personality traits which help make telecommuting successful. They look for people who value teamwork and co-operation but can work without constant human contact; they need to be flexible, able to ask for and provide support, and highly motivated. Established theories of work psychology break down personality characteristics into four main groups which describe key attributes of telecommuters:

Need for achievement
An individual who reports a high need for achievement is generally better able to complete a task within a certain time frame, to a higher degree of quality, without the support of co-workers and without the benefit of on-site supervision. Those who do not value achievement are less likely to meet targets set or to feel that self-discipline is necessary.

Need for autonomy
Those people who value the ability to choose the days of the week and the hours they work, and the tasks that are to be addressed as priorities, report that autonomy is very important to them. In effect, autonomous individuals prefer to choose and control their own working environment, timing and objectives within a very loose framework, rather than have these things imposed by a 'boss'. People who always wait to be told what to do rarely make successful telecommuters.

Need for order

A desire for order and structure is vital to the successful telecommuter. In the home environment, it is important that employees can work happily with the logic and order of a computer to gain primary information and set direction within work-related tasks. Such orderliness also helps when it comes to priorities that benefit both the company and the individual, and is particularly vital to the maintenance of a work schedule which allows for interruptions by family and neighbours but is still productive and not too frustrating.

Need for affiliation

The need to be with people is one of the more complex traits, which can work either with or against the telecommuter. It is important that home-workers should be productive and happy, despite the fact that they remain isolated in their daily work routine and have no contact with supervisors, co-workers, office structures (or traffic); but it is also essential that they remain aware of their role as a team-member and continue to take account of the needs and obligations of others. Whether high or low affiliation works best depends to a large extent on the organisational culture and support structures in place.

THE ORGANISATION'S POINT OF VIEW

Employees are only half the story when it comes to successful telecommuting. The way in which telecommuting is perceived, understood, dealt with and developed is highly dependent on the prevailing culture of the organisation, and inappropriate structures, hierarchies or beliefs can destroy a telecommuting programme before it even begins, irrespective of the enthusiasm of the employees.

Organisational culture

Organisational culture refers to the underlying beliefs, values and aspirations which underpin management practices and principles. These practices endure because they have meaning for members of an organisation, and represent strategies for survival that have worked well in the past. Such values, beliefs and meanings are the primary source of motivated and co-ordinated activity. In order for telecommuting to be embraced throughout an organisation, it is essential that it be perceived as a positive, constructive move rather than a negative one. In rigidly hierarchical companies, specific actions are often necessary for an individual to achieve promotion, and it may be difficult to carry out the required actions if one is not in the office. Other cultures equate high visibility with high performance, and promote accordingly. In different organisations, high value can be placed on one's office size, location and furnishings, rendering a home office very low on the list of achievements.

Telecommuting programmes flourish best in organisations that place less emphasis on power and status symbols, and more on teamwork, output and self-management. In such an environment, telecommuting can more readily be perceived by those who do it as a reward for their past successful performance, and something which will eventually lead to greater reward and recognition. If hierarchy and visibility are important, there is a risk that telecommuting will be perceived as a downward career move, taking the individual away from the office hub of activity.

The 'learning organisation'

Positive corporate cultures value experimentation and are prepared to take risks in order to gather more information about different types and styles of working. The 'learning organisation' is a term coined to express this attitude— essentially a corporate willingness to allow new approaches to be tested and the result stored and absorbed, whether good or bad. Learning organisations tend to be less hierarchical and less status-conscious than others, which provides great resilience to negative experiences: if 'failure' can be perceived as a learning experience as valid as 'success', it becomes easier to take risks. If power and status are not perceived as overwhelming priorities by and for employees, it becomes less of an issue if they are gained or lost by making a good or bad decision.

Organisations that make a success of telecommuting are able to learn from their own and others' mistakes, within the context of an open and supportive culture. Where, for instance, individuals are encouraged to allocate their own priorities and manage their own time accordingly, it is more likely that telecommuting will be perceived as a reward—a perk given in acknowledgement of mature and trustworthy behaviour, rather than a means to shuffle you off the promotion ladder. If recognition and reward become equated with performance and merit, rather than presence and politics, telecommuters stand as good a chance as anyone else of progressing their standing and salary within the organisation.

Organisations that are interested in starting or developing a telecommuting programme cannot afford to underestimate the importance of organisational culture and its impact on the way in which telecommuting is perceived by employees. A cultural audit, ideally performed by external consultants with no bias, can reveal trends, perceptions and beliefs among employees and managers which can lay the groundwork for success, but future growth depends on the maintenance of key cultural values by all employees:

- *Management* systems and methods must be *appropriate* to the flexible, distributed work environment that telecommuting requires and encourages.
- When people work at a distance from the core offices or from their functional base, a range of mechanisms and activities (regular phone calls, meetings and interactions) are important to keep them as *fully involved* as those who are still at the office every day. Workers who feel excluded in any sense from the mainstream of the enterprise can damage the morale of all telecommuters.
- It is foolish to do anything less than *take full advantage of the available technology*—with the basic technology of electronic mail widely used in less than 25 per cent of even the more telework-orientated companies, it is crazy

not to seize the technological initiative and get ahead.

- Technology is not just for telecommuters: better and more *widespread electronic links within and between office buildings* ensure that all employees are communicating at the same level with the same assumptions and understanding. Managed well, it is possible to develop an arrangement whereby the telecommuters become indistinguishable from the on-site employees.

POTENTIAL PROBLEMS FOR COMPANIES

Telecommuting is still something many organisations are reluctant to consider, no matter how progressive the culture. The reasons are varied but often derive from a poor understanding of the technology available and how it can be used, plus a fear that communication between important individuals will break down. Implementing a telecommuting programme will not be completely straightforward, but it is by no means as difficult or complicated as many nervous companies believe.

The technology is too unreliable/difficult/expensive

After years of widely reported IT disasters, many companies are understandably reluctant to make *more* new technology a central pivot of their growth strategy. Much of this comes down to limited awareness of developments in reliability and performance, which in turn can be attributed to ineffective and poorly co-ordinated marketing of the powerful and cheap global network services now in existence, and of the business opportunities which they present. Even so, compared to the USA, the costs of investing in a major new technological infrastructure are high. In Europe, for example, modems cost up to four times as much as their American equivalents and often comprise the single most expensive element of a home computer. UK users, therefore, are far more prepared to do without this peripheral and far less likely to develop an awareness of its potential. Overcoming this fear is the responsibility of both the suppliers of this technology and their customers: a gradual increase in the use of email within the office, for instance, will provide a 'taster' of good and useful technology which individual employees can be encouraged to follow up and 'champion' within their organisation.

Loss of management control

With employees out of sight and sound of their managers, appearing electronically only when required, it is hardly surprising that managers are worried about an erosion of their power-base. While the basic anxiety is justifiable, it can be much reduced, firstly, by accepting that the pace of technology in *all* respects will bring about cultural changes that will affect the role and duties of managerial staff. Telecommuting is just one such change and, because it is directly intended to provide greater flexibility for everyone, can be one of the most advantageous for managers. Once this is understood, it becomes easier to adapt to new requirements. For example, instead of managing a team of office-based employees, the primary task of the manager may become co-ordinating the delegation and collection of electronic work, plus the maintenance of communication between participating individuals. If this is also being done from home, the duties traditionally associated with the title 'manager' (providing leadership and organising meetings) become less relevant.

Many core managerial skills will remain important: goal-setting and monitoring, understanding personality and temperamental dynamics, and channelling the finished product to higher levels must still be done. The role may be less hierarchical, however: new managerial skills are likely to involve the tasks currently described as 'facilitating'. Instead of leading from the front, managers of telecommuters will add and gain more by increasing their involvement in the day-to-day tasks of employees and perhaps assuming their own share of the electronic workload. They will also be required to develop a better understanding of what is gained and lost by communicating electronically, and pace the extent to which individuals increase their 'at home' time. Timing, organising and focusing face-to-face meetings will be an important skill, as will an awareness of technology and its rate of change. Clearly, the role of the manager will not go away but will develop. Like everyone else, the most successful will be those who accept this and grow to accommodate changes, relinquishing out-of-date skills and trying to acquire new ones.

Breakdown of established communication channels

A real and valid concern of managers is that telecommuters will become isolated from the main body of office employees. Working remotely is seen as increasing the risk that communication will cease to flow either way, at both the formal work-orientated level and the equally important, personal level. Certainly, no good manager can afford to underestimate the importance of personal chat and gossip in creating bonds between individuals which outlast professional links.

The good news is that, like management skills, telecommuting will *change* the way people interact but will not remove their need or ability to do so—and the greater the number of telecommuters, the sooner a new electronic 'grapevine' will spring into life. Worries about a breakdown in communications also betray ineffective use of the available technology. A relatively modest investment of management effort, if led from the top, can correct this problem and will transform a company's responsiveness, whether or not it leads to development of telecommuting. To maximise communication, however, it is still important to encourage (or perhaps insist upon) regular face-to-face meetings between telecommuters. It is particularly crucial to facilitate meetings between new and existing members of a telecommuting team: technology can maintain existing relationships but is less good at forging new ones. Remember that telecommuting need not be all-or-nothing: it is entirely practicable to introduce it gradually, letting a few people work at home for perhaps two or three days a week, then adding others for longer periods as the organisation adapts.

Economic concerns (property rents, home-office maintenance)

The argument that telecommuting costs too much is simply groundless. Any increase in costs, such as the rent on 'empty' buildings, and the cost of setting up home-office workstations or retraining managers, will only ever be short term and should not be allowed to dictate telecommuting policy. In the short, medium and long term, telecommuting will at least balance expenditure and soon contribute to major cost savings. Apart from the direct savings to staff, who no longer have to pay the economic and social cost of physical commuting, there are marked economic advantages to organisations.

Most directly, fewer people in the office means lower office and premises costs. Indirect savings include a greater likelihood of retaining the skills of employees who might otherwise leave for domestic reasons, reducing or eliminating the cost of relocations, and gaining access to new labour markets. For the public-spirited, telecommuting can be viewed as a means to reduce traffic congestion and related pollution and environmental damage.

FACTORS THAT MAKE TELECOMMUTING WORK

In broad terms, the most important factors attributed to successful programmes are those that deal with human interaction: feelings of trust and support between the telecommuting employee and his or her manager, shared enthusiasm, and voluntary participation. The least important factors, on the other hand, are those that deal with the kind of control many organisations believe is necessary: observance of work rules, documenting results, tightly defined selection criteria, and management control. This is well worth knowing: even someone whose personality seems unsuited to telecommuting can contribute and remain productive if the interaction between her and her colleagues and managers remains positive, trusting and open.

Trust
There comes a point when you have to stop worrying about who is doing what where, and simply trust employees to manage their workloads. Managers report that trusting their off-site employees is the most important thing they can do to foster successful telecommuting. Such trust is critical where managers cannot oversee their employees and may have difficulty quantifying their work.

Enthusiasm and support
Because telecommuting is still an unusual practice in business, it will not succeed without a strong degree of enthusiasm, co-operation and support among all involved. If employees enjoy telecommuting, they are motivated to be highly productive, which in turn strengthens the trust between manager and employee.

Voluntary participation
Like any experiment into a significant new style of working, telecommuting will be received with caution or apprehension by many people. It is important to be aware of this and begin a programme only with those employees who have demonstrated a genuine interest in and enthusiasm for telecommuting. People forced into it against their wishes are unlikely to maintain the commitment required and may have greater difficulty overcoming the less appealing aspects of telecommuting, such as isolation and lack of motivation.

Programme availability
Making telecommuting available only to a selected number of employees can be important in the early stages of a programme. By doing this it is easier to monitor what is going on and to be sure that participants are enthusiastic and committed. Effective screening criteria can help to identify employees who are likely to have difficulty telecommuting for whatever reason: a lack of suitable work space at

home, maybe, or work which requires daily access to central files or equipment. Once the programme has become more widely accepted throughout the organisation, all employees should be given the option to telecommute. Results from some programmes suggest that telecommuting offers the possibility of transforming even marginal workers into key contributors.

Training
The early pioneers of a telecommuting programme can benefit from training, in their roles both as telecommuters and as managers of telecommuters. Particular areas to concentrate on are effective communication, management by objective, employee evaluation, time management, and the use of communication equipment. Additional areas of interest include aspects of entrepreneurship, motivation, and decision-making.

TELECOMMUTING STRATEGIES THAT WORK FOR EVERYONE

Employees can make it work by:

Selling it to the organisation
Your boss does not want to know how happy telecommuting will make *you*. When trying to get management buy-in, be sure to point out the advantages that will accrue to your employer, the organisation—*and* you. Firstly, the increase in flexibility which telecommuters gain is a direct route to greater happiness, greater control and significantly higher productivity. It is also sufficiently important to keep staff loyal and committed—if people are shown trust by employers, they are more likely to want to earn it. Lower staff turnover means reduced recruitment and training costs, and there is less risk of disrupting a cohesive team. The cost factor also helps here: although reductions in building rents are a long-term benefit, there are more immediate and observable benefits. If more than one person is telecommuting, it becomes possible to reduce the number of desks and

computers: employees can share, or 'hot-desk'. And with lower travelling and parking costs, employees are reaping financial benefits.

Focusing on quality, not quantity

Point out that you are hired to do a job, and define what the deliverables are for that job. Identify duties which can be performed at home (writing up reports, researching online databases, planning and creating) and acknowledge that some duties will still require office time (interviewing, presenting or meeting clients). Once you have identified home deliverables, point out the quality benefits that telecommuting will add to them, such as quicker turnaround time (fewer interruptions) and more thorough research (uninterrupted access to online information).

Defining your own goals

Don't wait for a reluctant manager to tell you what is required of you once you are working at home. Take the initiative by setting goals which *at least* match your output in the office, and be sure to make your point by comparing the two locations in terms of concrete deliverables. For instance, if you are normally required to analyse and summarise the implications of one financial spreadsheet a month, show that at home you could do two a month (or two every six weeks). If the workload cannot change to accommodate your new flexibility (if there is only one such spreadsheet a month), then define new goals you are now able to meet: maybe converting each report into a presentation; monitoring and compiling distribution lists for your report; or assuming additional responsibilities.

Creating your own communication targets

Offset worries about your sudden disappearance by committing yourself to as many interactions as seem appropriate (and feasible). Undertake to phone your group's secretary at least twice a day; promise to be by your phone between 10.00 am and 12.00 noon, no matter what; vow to attend that Monday morning meeting, however irrelevant you normally find it. And it goes without saying: always return messages left on your answerphone and always respond to email—*promptly*. A reputation for responsiveness, reliability and commitment will go a long way to selling your argument for telecommuting.

Starting gradually
Don't ask for everything at once. Meet your manager halfway and be prepared to compromise—if you want three days a week at home and you are offered two, accept them. Use those two days to produce high quality work, quickly, and let that make the case for you. Be in touch so regularly that your manager loses track of when you are in the office and when you are not; take the time to accumulate evidence that proves telecommuting works, then let it develop from there.

Becoming totally mobile
Stress that telecommuting does not mean just that you have relocated your desk from office to home: do your best to gain access to a notebook computer and demonstrate that, if necessary, you can telecommute on the road as well. Practise making modem connections from home and in hotel rooms, and make the effort to learn a little about what is actually happening when you dial in to the office network or a remote service (see Chapter 5). This way the distinctions between when you are working and when you are not become far less obvious to employers—or perhaps more importantly, you gain far greater control over when you want to be available and when you don't.

Identifying a contact
Ideally you should keep in touch with everyone you interact with at work when you are out of the office. In reality, however, it will not work like that—some people are better than others at returning calls, some are away from their desks more often and others are uncomfortable about chatting when they feel they should be working. Counteract the drop in general conversation by identifying a specific

individual who can become your eyes and ears while you are at home. If you are lucky, you may have a secretary whose job is to do exactly that; perhaps you have a subordinate or colleague, with similar duties to yours, who can keep you up to date. If there is no obvious professional contact you can call regularly, establish an informal one—a friend in the next office, a coffee partner or colleague from an earlier project, perhaps. Obviously it is most useful if your contact can supply relevant professional information as well as the latest grapevine intrigues, but do not underestimate the value of gossip as a source of information—office relationships have an inevitable effect on professional outcomes. The more closely you can keep in touch with your colleagues, at whatever level, the better informed and more in control you will be. You could pre-empt the boss yet.

Cultivating the gurus

If your organisation is prepared to support even an experimental telecommuting programme, the chances are that there is a reasonably sophisticated information technology infrastructure already in place. Make a point of getting to know the people who are paid to understand and maintain this infrastructure, and make use of their skills and knowledge. They can help you connect better, and get on and off the network remotely. If your company does not have an expert in these matters, be prepared to assume the mantle yourself and promote telecommuting within your company.

Promoting and discussing

Once you are telecommuting, itemise and demonstrate the benefits, then talk about them—to your employer, your colleagues and your friends. The arguments against telecommuting are not that strong—while some jobs require presence, many do not, and almost none require total and uninterrupted presence. Your enthusiasm, plus demonstrable personal and corporate gains, will become highly persuasive factors for others already supporting or considering instigating a telecommuting programme in their own organisations.

Employers can make it work by:

Introducing it gradually
The beauty of telecommuting is that it lends itself to evolution (or, perhaps, caution)—there is no need to rush into it or force employees to participate if they are not ready. The introduction of telecommuting can be gradual in terms of both *which individuals* are participating and *to what extent* they are participating. Many organisations already support informal telecommuters without feeling that they are committed to a full-scale telecommuting programme. It is perfectly reasonable to allow informal arrangements to emerge naturally until positive benefits become apparent, or until management staff are sufficiently happy to develop a formal strategy to introduce telecommuting.

Beginning with self-selected, motivated employees
The benefits of telecommuting will become most apparent most quickly with people who are keen to participate and who perceive the chance to telecommute as a tremendous opportunity. Such people will present far fewer problems for managers, are more likely to resolve technical or scheduling problems on their own initiative and are better able to persuade others of the benefits of what they are doing.

Re-evaluating methods of employee measurement
Without even realising it, many managers evaluate the commitment and performance of their employees by monitoring how often they are physically present; in many cases, a high profile is an essential step towards promotion. Whilst visibility *is* important for high status management positions, it is less important for jobs which focus on converting managerial strategies into actual work. Telecommuters need to be evaluated on the quality of their work: accuracy, thoroughness, speed and hitting deadlines, for example, rather than how hard they appear to be working. High fliers need not be excluded from telecommuting: so long as it is understood on both sides that high levels of recognition are important to the effective performance of their duties, there

is no reason why they should not set aside time during the week when their main goal is simply to be seen and heard by colleagues.

Making meetings and communication a priority

Effective teams are composed of members who know and understand each other. Encourage telecommuters to meet and chat with one another on a regular basis to build up the closeness and familiarity which oil the wheels of a productive team. If members of a team are working different days away from the office and cannot easily get to one another, make a weekly meeting compulsory, at least to begin with. Good telecommuters are good time managers—there is no reason why they cannot make such a commitment.

Not quibbling over trivial costs

Telecommuting introduces new costs to an organisation and there are many unexplored issues concerning lighting, heating and telephone bills which worry employers. It is foolish, however, to jeopardise a potentially long-term cost-saving, productivity-raising exercise by quibbling over minor increases of this nature. Offset increases in outgoings against the substantial savings to be gained in the short term by greater productivity and better staff retention, and in the long term through direct trade-offs: lower office rents, heating, lighting and telephone bills. Also bear in mind that you can reduce phone bills by setting up 0800 numbers for staff dialling into the office network, and many online databases also offer this facility.

WOMEN WITH CHILDREN—A SPECIAL CASE?

In the politically correct 1990s there is no reason why women should be responsible for child care any more than men. In practice, however, child care is still largely the responsibility of women and the fact remains that it is women who actually give birth and undergo the disruption such an event can cause to their careers. It is not unusual for even a relatively short period of maternity leave to set a woman's career back years, as she loses touch with colleagues, skills and office politics. This, coupled with the additional demands a small child places on time and energy, can substantially reduce a woman's professional effectiveness.

Telecommuting is often perceived as an ideal solution for women who wish to maintain fulfilling careers without neglecting their children; indeed, a large percentage of tele-workers are women with young children who have chosen this option to obtain a more 'holistic' experience of work and motherhood. Work and home life, they say, can be reintegrated, and the responsibilities of child care reconciled with the needs and pleasures of work. In many ways, tele-commuting *is* the best compromise a committed employee can hope for, but it is not necessarily a means of attaining the best of both worlds.

To draw a direct comparison, there are few people who would perform as effectively if they brought a young child into the office every day. Quite apart from the impact this would have on other employees, the demands of a child have scant respect for meetings, telephone calls or general pro-fessionalism. On the other hand, if you can control your own hours of work, and if you are no longer dependent on a lengthy journey in to your workplace, it is easier to vary your work schedule and to switch back as needed into your parental role. There are more opportunities to take time off for dental or medical visits, and routine school runs become more plausible. It is important to recognise that achieving a balance requires planning and negotiation, wherever your office may be, and it is likely to include some form of organised child care arrangement.

Negotiating with employers

A telecommuting arrangement will not on its own resolve child care problems: it is important that a woman and her employer agree on the terms and conditions of her telecom-muting. To begin with, it is important that the corporate cultural factors are in place, whereby telecommuting does not come to mean demotion or out-of-the-picture. Until it is possible for anyone to suggest telecommuting without risking their career, it will be difficult to make it work well for women. American corporations were condemned in the Eighties for introducing the 'Mommy Track', an official, slow promotion career path for women who wanted to have children—overtly forcing women to choose between family and professional success. The rise in single parent families (most of which are female-headed) has also contributed to perceptions in some areas that women who telecommute are different and somehow of less value than men who telecommute.

Negotiation with employers must start with the premise that telecommuting is a viable, flexible working arrangement of benefit to everyone, rather than a favour to the employee—this is something that must be understood by everyone involved. New mothers need to take into account their physical and emotional state after birth, and ensure that they take their full entitlement of maternity leave. Being at home does not mean telework must start immediately; on the contrary, it is important that it does not creep into official maternity leave. The same goes for annual leave: these precious days will be required for other things, and should not be soaked up by telecommuting.

Career options for the future

It's always a good idea to begin by stating clearly what you would like to happen in terms of your career once you have begun to raise a family. Be positive and plan ahead, but always bear in mind that your needs and aspirations might change.

Short term
If you are anxious to return full time to the activity of your office after a short period at home with the baby, you should present telecommuting as a short-term option intended to provide maximum convenience to you and your employer. Specify dates and conditions: for one thing, you need to be certain that a desk will be waiting for you when you

return! This short-term option may make it difficult for your employer to justify investing in computer equipment for your home office: suggest instead that you use a notebook or other portable PC which can be returned to your employer when you return to the office; or be prepared to invest in your own equipment.

Medium to long term

Children are often the trigger for women to rethink their career objectives and seek a more flexible working life. Formerly, this meant missing out on significant career opportunities, but now the chance to telecommute can mean the chance to spend more time at home without giving up the fulfilment and opportunities of a career. Making such arrangements requires preparation similar to that required by anyone considering telecommuting, and implies that the same organisational and managerial factors must be in place in order to make it work. Babies will not wait for managers to make up their minds, however. If your organisation is not culturally receptive to telecommuting, you may find that your wishes are perceived as an attempt to reduce your working hours or your influence and role within the company.

If this is the case, there will be far more pressure on you to sell the concept and prove that it can work. Recruit supporters from amongst your colleagues and present a watertight argument to the boss, whose co-operation and support will be essential to your success. Many of the points listed above apply equally to everyone; women with children need only point out the additional benefits their employer will gain: a two-year break is a relatively short period in the context of a long and productive career, and a generally more flexible working life will confer the same benefits of loyalty, flexibility and greater commitment.

If there is initial resistance or caution you may need to put in more work hours than you would normally expect, simply to make the point, but do not fall into the trap of routinely working harder than before because it has become expected of you. If your employer (or you) have unrealistic expectations of what you will be able to do, everyone will be disappointed. Make it clear that telecommuting is a way to *maintain* your commitment and productivity during a difficult physical and emotional adjustment, not a means of doubling your output in half the time.

Be clear about what you want to achieve and what you are prepared to put into the job. For instance, if you have achieved the status and position you want, your goal should be to continue doing that well. If you are ambitious and keen to earn promotion, state overtly that these are your intentions and work towards them. Bear in mind that more senior managerial positions are likely to require more time in the office and greater involvement in the broader issues of the organisation—you may need to sacrifice at-home time to achieve this. Most likely is that telecommuting will allow you to keep up with your original duties whilst also enabling you to consider other, more 'horizontal', options. For instance, your job may require you to be in the office three days a week in the normal scheme of things. As a telecommuter, things may work better if you swap some duties with a colleague, assuming responsibility for sections of their computer work whilst they become more involved in face-to-face meetings with your clients. This may not put you in line for divisional manager, but it will fit in better with your needs whilst ensuring that necessary jobs get done well.

7 Growing Your Business

Whatever the scale of your proposed (or actual) home-working endeavours, there will come a point when you must decide exactly what it means to you. Unless you are telecommuting—that is, working at home for an employer—you will not be receiving a salary and you will have no employer to make the effort if things start to slide. So, is it just a hobby, where the point is not to make money but to occupy yourself? Is it something you enjoy, so long as the workload is manageable and does not take up more valuable socialising time? Or is it something you see as a potentially serious business and the main source of income in your life, where you can foresee yourself actively seeking out new clients, developing formal tax and accounting structures, maybe recruiting staff—and putting everything else in your life second?

Much of this depends on the goals you should have set yourself earlier (see Chapter 6) and exactly what your priorities in life are. Other important factors include the financial resources you already have (do you *need* to work for a living or is a partner's salary adequate?) and the feelings and support levels of other family members. Whatever you want to achieve, however, it is likely that at some point, unless you really only want a hobby, you will want to advertise your services in the hope of increasing or regenerating your business. How do you go about this?

ONLINE MARKETING

Advertising in local newspapers, Yellow Pages or trade magazines is a useful way to start publicising your skills, but this book is about the technology that is available to the small office and home office. For the shrewd computer user there is a vast range of electronic marketing options, many of which are quicker and cheaper than conventional methods, and capable of reaching an infinitely wider audience. Before you plunge into exploring them, however, a word of warning. Electronic dial-in services, also known as 'cyberspace' (particularly the Internet), still represent largely uncharted territory and, despite the recent leap of such services into the spotlight, have not matured into a medium which can be made useful immediately, particularly if you have never used them before. It can be difficult to navigate your way around the Internet and related services, and difficult to find useful and relevant information. More to the point, perhaps, is the very large amount of poor quality information on it. Because the Internet is almost totally unregulated, it is open literally to anyone who wants to use it. So while there is a lot of good and interesting material there, there is also a lot of rubbish.

Nonetheless, because so many people are 'cruising' the Net, the potential for businesses advertising on there (or on similar services) is almost indescribably immense. 'Cyberspace' is a far more interactive medium than a newspaper, with a strongly upheld etiquette ('netiquette' for the initiated) enforced by highly computer-literate and opinionated users. Activity is unregulated, with a cultural suspicion of commercial activity which derives from its non-commercial roots. There are undoubtedly hazards associated with putting publicity material on the so-called information superhighway, but that has always been the case when a powerful tool becomes available. By doing your homework and respecting the protocol of this vast new medium, there are rich rewards to be reaped from high-tech advertising and marketing in cyberspace.

Before you switch on and fire up your modem, bear in mind that this chapter is not a step-by-step guide to the actual process of marketing on the Internet. If you are already a user of online services treat this chapter as a source of marketing ideas and pointers. If you are a complete beginner, you will probably benefit from a live introduction to the Internet from an Internet service provider or a knowledgeable friend—alternatively, there are plenty of books available which give more detailed information about the Internet itself.

WHERE DO I BEGIN?

Chapter 4 explains the basics of the existing online services and some of the ways in which they are being used. The Internet is the largest network of computers in the world, and most other networked computer services are in some way linked to it. They may be a sub-set of the Internet (for example, Usenet Newsgroups), or proprietary services which are connected to it by an electronic 'gateway' (for example, CompuServe). The point is that wherever you place your electronic message, the chances are it will be seen by Internet users eventually, so you may as well make the most of the opportunities this provides. Repositories for marketing information within the Internet include thousands of bulletin boards, forums and email.

Before you start, it is well worth 'lurking' (that is, reading threads of conversation without participating) to get a feel for the tone and depth of interaction in areas relevant to your interests. You will also pick up some rudimentary 'netiquette' which will help you avoid later disasters. As an entity, the Internet is still a relatively esoteric creature and largely remains the province of those 'netsurfers' who are very comfortable with technology. For the rest of us, there are some key areas of the Internet where significant time and effort have been devoted to making information far more accessible to 'ordinary' users. The Internet as a marketing tool can be a frightening prospect—huge, globe-spanning and populated by all sorts of weirdos—but don't worry, you are not about to start exposing your poor little back bedroom to the scrutiny of everyone who ever owned a modem. The first thing you need to do is identify areas of the Internet—or areas which are linked to the Internet—where you can usefully interact, and unless you are already a serious netsurfer, there are really only two: CompuServe and the World-Wide Web.

CompuServe

CompuServe is one of the most mature bulletin board systems and also one of the fastest-growing. It is separate from the Internet, but as mentioned in Chapter 4, a gateway now exists between the two such that email can pass between them, and it is also possible to view Internet forums from Compu-Serve. Its great advantage is its usability and reliability, both products of its relative age and the fact that it is privately owned and maintained (by CompuServe). Technical and networking skills are simply not required to use Compu-Serve (unlike many areas of the Internet, where a passing familiarity with network protocols and baud rates comes in handy). Like the Internet, CompuServe is composed of forums covering a wide range of interests, although its bias is perhaps slightly more commercial and technical. It is a well populated service, and tends to have a large proportion of users whose interest in computing is secondary to their interest in the subject matter of the forums in which they participate.

For the small business which really wants no more than a manageable flow of work, CompuServe is the best place to start. There is no strong marketing culture there, and you will not run into any heavyweight advertisers or professional marketing activity. What is greatly preferred by participants and managers is a far subtler approach—generally you will find that the 'atmosphere' mimics an informal leisure environment rather than a commercial one, the aim being a genuine flow of information between interested individuals rather than any sort of hard sell. Marketing activity is kept well away from the main forums—either in specific libraries where information can be uploaded and read by people who actually want it; or within the CLASSIFIEDS section.

First steps to generating business online: marketing without the marketing

Because of its easy-to-understand interface, navigation through CompuServe is simple and productive and you will find you quickly pick up the basics. Start by joining forums of interest and then gradually join in the conversations already under way. Introducing yourself as a potential service-provider can begin with a modest mention as part of an informal conversation with other users within a forum or discussion group. If you phrase your words appropriately and stick to forums where there are likely to be participants who have a natural interest in whatever it is you are offering, you will find plenty of opportunities to mention your services. This may generate requests for further information, word-of-mouth (or keyboard) recommendation and a small but steady flow of business. This could be all you need.

A lot of people swear by this 'natural' networking approach and many forum managers (sysops) prefer and encourage it in favour of anything more commercial. Forum participation becomes simply an electronic grapevine whereby your reputation and abilities become known gradually, through your regular participation, willingness to help and informed opinion on relevant matters. If you are too overt about pushing your product, however, the response will be less favourable: introduce it inappropriately, or mention price and delivery information unasked, and you may find yourself the recipient of cold-shouldering, curt messages from the sysops or even multiple mail bombs. Repeat offenders are mercilessly banned from forums. Online users are acutely aware of commercial opportunists and will not spare you if you are caught marketing on the sly. A slightly more formal approach might include uploading marketing literature about yourself into specified areas (libraries), which are clearly marked as commercial areas. That way, you will get a narrower readership but one which is looking for marketing information and knows what to expect.

Create your own section

Once you are a more familiar figure within a given forum,

you will stand more chance of setting up your own section—or even becoming a sysop yourself. Anyway, for your business to stand any chance of survival, you must have established that there is an existing audience for what you are offering—rather than getting people to attend to your direct messages, encourage them to talk about the subject naturally by creating an area where people with this intrinsic interest can discuss their own points of view. At the simplest level, you could set up a separate discussion area (or thread) within an existing forum, which will have a natural lifespan of anywhere between three days and three months, depending on the number of interested participants. The content of threads can be of variable quality, but at least you create an opportunity to introduce relevant background issues and encourage participants to browse through additional information you may have available.

Building up a business base using non-aggressive, networking methods can take longer than by placing direct advertisements. However, the work you do get tends to be exactly what you want, from clients who understand and respect your expertise and will be more than happy to recommend you to others. Once a momentum begins you may find you have no further need for advanced online marketing. On the other hand . . .

ADVANCED ONLINE MARKETING

If you are deadly serious about your business, have ambitious expansion plans and a carefully thought-out approach to marketing—in which you are prepared to invest money—you may find CompuServe too informal for your needs. If so, the next step is the Internet itself, where there is almost no regulation, less discernible 'atmosphere' (although selling is still generally regarded with distaste) and far less help for 'newbies' (newcomers). Marketing on the Internet is more difficult, but potentially more rewarding—if you get it right. Most people will want to begin with the World-Wide Web.

World-Wide Web

The World-Wide Web is a sector of the Internet especially organised to handle information requests. It is a network of servers like the rest of the Internet, but, as we saw in Chapter 4, has one unique difference: it can handle text, pictures, sound and video, whereas all other Internet services are limited to text only. Access to the Web is via a 'browser', literally a piece of graphical software enabling you to browse through the information stored there. Mosaic and Netscape are the two main browsers, and their intensely graphical orientation makes the Web one of the easiest, most intuitive and attractive areas of the Internet. The Web uses a 'magazine' metaphor—that is, it is designed so that information is presented rather like the pages of a magazine. Words, phrases or pictures can provide a link to other pages which provide more information relevant to that word, phrase or picture (in this paragraph, for example, the word 'Web' could lead to another page providing introductory information to the Web). Link-words are a different colour from ordinary words and become active (take the user to a new page) when you click with a mouse on the word.

Create your own Web page
Not for the faint-hearted, the creation of your own Web page is probably one of the most effective marketing techniques you can undertake, because once it is there, it is easy for other people to get to, and attractive (and interactive) to view. Like many aspects of computer (and Internet) technology, getting started and setting up a *very basic* page is surprisingly easy; what is difficult is doing it well and thoroughly. Using the Web assumes you have access via browser software, typically Netscape or Mosaic; once you are browsing you are well under way. Discuss setting up your own Web page with your Internet provider who will know the rudiments of set-up and may even provide you with some space on a server plus a Unique Resource Locator (URL)—effectively a Web address. You will also need some familiarity with the Web's HyperText Markup

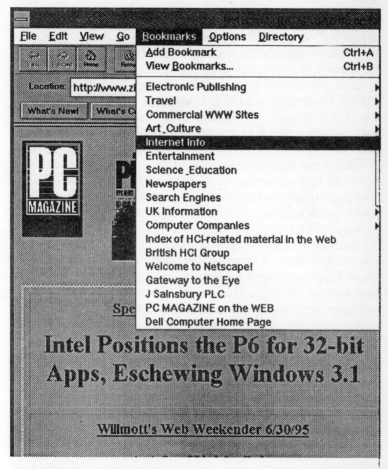

A Web page of PC Magazine, *showing the issue's latest features in an attractive and accessible format. It is easy to move from one page to another by clicking the mouse or using the pull-down menus. Pages you visit frequently can be stored as 'Bookmarks' so that you can get back to them easily.*

Language (html) in which Web pages are written. As preparation, you can trawl through the Web looking up existing URLs which explain basic techniques for setting up a Web page: established Netscape users can drop in on http://www.ncsa.uiuc.edu.demoweb.html-primer.html to start learning.

If this sounds too much to cope with (and it is by no means straightforward if you are new to cyberspace), there are growing numbers of people who will create a page for you—if you can't find them yourself by just browsing, your Internet provider will have a plentiful list of people who will do this. Bear in mind that to make the most of your page, you will need to be sufficiently comfortable with the Web to respond to interested enquiries promptly and effectively— don't get a page set up and then discover you do not know how to find it or use it.

A single Web page can accommodate all the text you need, wrapped around pictures, photographs or illustrations. Your company logo (if you have one), a picture of your product or a sample of your service can all be made available, along with single-click access to your email address. For anything more complex, such as an electronic order form or other interactive tool which requires email traffic, you will be adding considerable costs. Order forms are useful and can be extremely effective in getting people to request your services immediately, but you need to cover the costs of the management, server space and email traffic you will require of your Internet provider. Because the Web can be so effective, think carefully about the amount you are prepared to spend and the return you need to make.

HOW TO GET YOUR MESSAGE ACROSS

Online marketing basics

If you feel that the service you and your computer can offer is ready to expand, there are some marketing basics which must be put in place before you even think about taking out a subscription to the Internet. Before you even switch on your modem, start your marketing campaign well in advance by preparing a battery of *information tools*. You may prefer an article to a press release; or feel that a small advertisement is all you need to get your message across. Whatever level you are aiming at, you should give yourself maximum flexibility by creating a range of information tools which can be unleashed on an unsuspecting usership as and when appropriate. Information tools are essentially computer files of any type (text, graphics; a report or book, short video clip) which contain information about your product or service. This could be a snippet of direct explanation, a series of facts about areas related to what you do, or a short demonstration of your product's capabilities. Your tools need not all be used at once; use them gradually and experimentally and concentrate on what works best.

Unsurprisingly, the basics of marketing hold as true for cyberspace as they do for billboards, small ads and television campaigns: first and foremost, *you must have something worthwhile to sell*. The people who use the Internet are the same people who drive around towns and watch television, and they are as likely to be irritated by a poorly planned advertisement on the Net as they are by one on television. The difference is that on the Net they can do something about it—offending users are 'flamed' by others, a process whereby hundreds or thousands of meaningless mail messages are sent to the originator's mailbox until it becomes blocked and useless. So prepare to greet your new audience with some caution and make sure you undertake the following preparation:

Preparing your online message
A need for marketing does not imply a natural understanding of the subject, which is something all entrepreneurs realise—eventually. If you want to run your own show, you have to do everything from writing the business plan to making the coffee; in short, you have to patch together enough knowledge to cope with all aspects of generating and sustaining work. Marketing is just one of these aspects.

Online marketing corresponds most closely with direct mail marketing, in that you are using information to persuade specific (targeted) individuals at a long distance to buy your product or service. As such, it makes sense to pay attention to some of the fundamental rules of successful direct marketing. For a start, you need to create AIDA:

Attention: start the ball rolling by grabbing the attention of your audience. Something controversial ('All software is a waste of time!'); provocative ('Need to impress someone?') or intriguing ('Don't read this!') will usually catch the eye, but beware of overdoing it. Blatant or overt attention-seizing tactics which prove groundless ('SEX! has nothing to do with this advertisement but now that you're here read on . . .') are irritating and will make your readers feel conned. They will become annoyed with themselves for falling for such a crass trick and take their annoyance out on you—by moving swiftly on.

Interest: Once you have the ear (or eye) of your potential customer, build interest. On the Internet, interest means information, and a reader whose attention has been attracted wants that attraction explained. Provide information to explain to your reader why he or she is reading: describe your service or product and, if it is appropriate, focus on a single point or feature which is of particular relevance to the people you want to buy. If you are a lawyer with a special knowledge of broadcast media, you are particularly keen to build the interest of people involved with television and radio. You are probably advertising on media-related forums to begin with, so there is an intrinsic interest anyway. Take advantage by focusing again on your unique offering and how it can benefit the people you are trying to reach.

Desire: interest isn't enough; your public has to want—to desire—what you have got to offer. Build on the interest you have already found by focusing on a specific point or area. Dwell on your product's exclusivity, usefulness to a particular professional group, or importance to a certain style of living. Desire means getting emotionally involved with what is available, getting people to want it or believe that it is truly important and necessary to them.

Action: they are gasping for your services—make sure there is a way out for them. Supply, clearly and unambiguously, a point of contact for further details, an order or just a chat. Ideally your Internet address, but a telephone number or address as well if you want to encourage unfamiliar users or locals who may prefer to use the phone to get in touch with you. Alternatively, you could refer them to a further point of information, such as a forum or discussion where you are regularly active, an existing satisfied customer, or a report you have uploaded. Encourage readers to take the action you suggest, perhaps by specifying times when you are definitely online and keen to talk.

Successful marketing: what to do

Focus on marketing in fewer, more productive areas
If you are serious about generating new business electronically, you have to know who is online and where they are. The users of online services are far less well defined than, say, the viewers of a certain television programme, and they are also changing more rapidly as more and more people dip a toe in the murky waters of the Internet. Whittle down your 'hit zone' by identifying the Forums and Special Interest Groups (SIGs) which might be relevant to what you are offering: start simply by using the 'Find' command to trawl through CompuServe or the Web looking for keywords. Once you have identified a core of relevant groups (it may be only four or five) you will quickly find references to other groups if you need them, since many people with a particular interest are members of many related forums and will talk about these areas during normal interactions online.

The important thing is that you don't start by tackling the Internet as a single, amorphous, globe-spanning mass—such an exercise would be far too daunting for even the largest corporation. Start with a handful of localised areas, maybe just on CompuServe or the Web, where you feel comfortable, where you can be more certain that the kind of person you want will be participating, and where a marketing project will be manageable. There is little point in generating requests and orders for your expertise from around the world if you would rather just supply a little consultancy to a client set only slightly larger than immediate friends and family.

Focus on products that sell well online

Exhaustive and far-reaching though it is, cyberspace has not penetrated every corner of the world—nor every back bedroom. There is a bias in the type of person you'll find online which means that some products will sell significantly better than others. For a start, regular Internet users must have regular access to a computer and modem, which implies a better-than-average living standard and level of education. The existing research suggests that the 'typical' Net user (or the closest there is to 'typical') is a relatively affluent professional in a well paid job. Of these, there is a high proportion who make their living from computers in some way—designing, programming, training or developing—and many others involved in running their own businesses with the aid of technology. The bias is firmly towards the information industries, though, so it is hardly surprising that information-orientated products sell best. Writing (usually technical rather than creative), programming, training, and consultancy are typical information-orientated services, whilst software, books and CD-ROMs are popular products. If you are selling lawnmower spares or offering cat and dog holiday homes, you may find business on the Internet disappointing. Don't be entirely discouraged, however—florists and pizza delivery companies seem to have made a comfortable living for themselves online. Hungry programmers placating their spouses, perhaps?

Create basic marketing documents

Once you know what you can offer to whom, and where, you can prepare the communications material you will need to be most effective. The simplest document is probably a short announcement of your product or service in the form of a classified advertisement; or you could begin with a press release, report or sales letter.

CompuServe is perhaps the best place to start—contact the sysops (systems operators) of your preferred forums for advice about how and where to place material, and you could be pleasantly surprised by the extent and helpfulness of their advice. These knowledgeable individuals expect and encourage enquiries from forum participants, and even if you blunder into the wrong place, will usually put you right.

Test it!
Once you have prepared something appropriate to your services, start small. One placement of your material in the forum you think most relevant will give you a feel for the type and volume of response you can expect and an idea of how you want to proceed. If you begin to receive enquiries by email, by all means respond with a full onslaught of marketing literature—but not otherwise. The great thing about online marketing is the speed with which you can expect to receive feedback—your experimental marketing can yield results within hours, irrespective of what time you place an ad. All these online services are used twenty-four hours a day around the world and there is no need to worry about postage. Of course you may prefer to keep your business more local, in which case you can either specify this in your documentation or concentrate on forums with a specific local slant (UK Professionals on CompuServe, for example).

Successful marketing: what *not* to do

Don't send unsolicited email
Don't, whatever you do, send unsolicited email to strangers, even if you are certain the recipients would be interested. For serious Net users, unexpected marketing mail is perceived as an ugly commercial intrusion into their wacky cyberlives and an open invitation to them to start flaming you. This ghastly crime breaches the most sacred netiquette and lays you open to large volumes of hostile replies. Requesting an automatic

receipt (for your market research) will also be perceived as a calculated and predatory gesture—you will appear to be checking up on your prospects who will assume you are planning a further assault, and may take pre-emptive action. If you are lucky, this will be limited to a request to send no further mail—a normal response will be some fairly blunt messages asking you to desist; and if you are unlucky, an Internet provider sympathetic to your prospect's annoyance may cut off your Internet account. So don't do it.

Don't focus on yourself at the expense of your customers
It is very tempting to fill your marketing information with details of yourself, your skills and your long record of creativity/reliability or punctuality; indeed, in many cases this information will be required and appropriate. If you are trying to generate new business, however, such information can leave prospective clients thinking 'so what?' and may be perceived as selfish, or worse, irrelevant. Much more effective are marketing tools that focus on the client and how his or her needs can be met by you. Not only do prospective customers gain far more interesting and relevant information this way, they also recognise that you have thought about them and their needs. This applies equally to your informal discussions in forums with peers—what are *they* interested in?

Don't start marketing without defining your market
With the entire Net before you, it is easy to believe that the 'shotgun approach' will be more than adequate to get you new business: by scattering your information tools all over the place, sooner or later someone will get in touch with you. There is some truth in this, but it can have its downsides. You may get requests from people whose needs you simply cannot meet through time or resource constraints; new orders may call upon skills you don't really have and don't plan to acquire; you may find yourself getting distracted from your real objective in order to meet the needs of clients who are not stretching you or enhancing your reputation in the area you want to develop.

You will have a lot more control over the kind of requests you get if you take the trouble to find out a little about the kind of person or organisation for whom your product or service is most relevant. If you are offering account management services to small businesses, your marketing effort should start with some research into exactly *who* these small businesses are. Are they, for example, middle-aged executives with a solid career behind them who want to branch out on their own? Are they bright young things with an entrepreneurial spirit but no real capital? Are they primarily service- or product-orientated concerns? Find out. Depending on what stage you have already reached, decide what you *want* your market *to be* (by evaluating your own skills and deciding where they can be most effectively applied), or review what your market *already is* by researching your existing client base. Define the skills you have and the clients who need them, and concentrate on these. Time enough for the odd stray or experimental project when you are more firmly established in your field.

Don't start marketing without a clear idea of what you want to achieve
Following on from the above, a poorly planned approach to online marketing can land you in deep trouble. Because they are so new, the power of the online services is easy to under(or over)estimate, and a concerted effort could bring in a completely unexpected response: more—or less—business than you can handle, of the wrong kind, from the wrong clients, in the wrong area. Minimise the problems to you and everyone who reads your literature by deciding exactly what it is you want your marketing effort to achieve. Do you want just one extra client? Write a list of clients you would like and target them, one at a time. Do you want to add a client a month? Stick to relevant forums and pace your marketing to enable you to cope with that rate of growth. Do you want to add as many new customers as you possibly can as soon as possible? Be sure you have the resources to cope if this occurs. Stick to marketing that will achieve your goals as well as those of your customers and potential customers.

Be realistic and keep it steady, and expect to negotiate over email in the same way that you would in normal circumstances. Be prepared to travel to face-to-face meetings when necessary and build that into your marketing. Do not target Hong Kong, for example, if a flight there would bankrupt you.

Don't lose opportunities to gather name and address data
Maintain a formal, organised approach to people who respond to your marketing. Give them what they ask for, be it further information, a chat, or even a real order, but don't let them melt back into the ether once you have satisfied that initial enquiry. Keep a record of names, addresses, email addresses and the nature of the enquiry every time you interact: people who have already shown an interest are far more likely to show it again when they see your name (assuming you performed well the first time). This information will form the basis of a valuable business tool—your customer list. Immediately, it becomes a mailing list of people who have expressed a definite interest in your services and from whom future enquiries are a strong prospect. Use it to invite people to participate in your forum if you have one; or simply to join in with a (relevant) discussion in which you are interested. Use it to send them your newsletter, or to send some sort of hint or tip that will help them and demonstrate your strengths. Use it to tell them about discounts or offers, to direct them to your Web page.

All this can be useful, but beware—you are treading a thin line between solicited and unsolicited mail. Make it clear in your first posting that you are sending information because *they expressed an interest* earlier and be sure to tell them what to do if they *no longer* wish to receive information. Don't make them take action if they *do* want to keep receiving information—a lot of people simply won't bother even if they're interested, so put the onus on them to cancel your postings. If someone does explicitly request that you remove them from a mailing list, do so—at once. Satisfied customers and interested readers will always be happy to hear from you, so concentrate your efforts on keeping them sweet, rather than on building a long list of people who won't bother to look twice and will probably just get annoyed.

Don't lose opportunities to offer other services that might be useful

Just because someone makes use of one part of your skill set does not mean they have no use for another part. Be proactive in your dealings with customers and always look for an opportunity to suggest other ways in which you can help them. This is not being pushy, it is an example of knowing exactly who they are and what they want from you: a client who has been concentrating on one need may not be monitoring other requirements so closely—take it upon yourself to keep an eye on his needs and remind him what else would be of benefit. He may simply be unaware that you are offering other things, or not have realised how well you would fit in with other plans, so take every chance you can to explain about new skills you have acquired or relevant experiences you have had, always within the context of his needs and desires. And of course, always say thank you for the business.

Don't make doing business with you difficult

Unless your customers are fanatical about you or riveted by your literature, they will give up if you are difficult to find, frequently unobtainable or do not have the answers they need right away. Provide lavish amounts of contact information when encouraging interested readers to take action: list email address, real address and names. One telephone number minimises confusion, but if you need to, list a main number, alternative number, day and evening numbers, mobile numbers, fax numbers. Specify hours of availability—and the nearer you can get to twenty-four, the better. Do not even start soliciting business without a telephone answering machine or voicemail system: on your messages, provide reassurance that callers are through to the right number by stating the same name they will have read in the literature, and encourage them to leave a message and their contact details. Always call back, and always be prepared: schedule periods when you take and make phone calls, preferably when you have ready access to your company's background data. The impressiveness of a prompt response is badly offset if you cannot tell a new client when you will be able to meet him, because your diary's in the office and you are on the road.

ONCE YOUR BUSINESS IS STABLE . . .

Online newsletters

If you are happy with the customers you have and simply want to retain them, or the nature of your services means that you may not see clients more than once or twice a year, you may wish simply to keep in touch. Maintaining a loyal customer base is every bit as important as increasing your client list, and for many small businesses is all that is required to keep them ticking over at a rate that keeps the money coming in without working you into the ground. If that describes you, the best marketing option may be a simple electronic newsletter—or even a paper printout through the post!—dispatched to everyone in your business address book two or three times a year.

A newsletter need not be ambitious—two pages (around one thousand words) is plenty to get your message across without boring your readers. An electronic version needs a strong and eye-catching headline or title to distinguish it from other text files, and a number of short, snappy articles will be read with greater tolerance and interest than a single solid chunk of text. In terms of content, concentrate on what is of interest to your clients: they will only be interested in reading about *your* profit and loss if they have still got important business with you which relies on your staying afloat for the next six months. Far better to dwell on how your services can affect *their* bottom line—remind them how useful your efforts can be by citing case studies (with permission); excerpting relevant research documents (gleaned online, of course); and demonstrating any additional new services or facilities you are now offering. Although humour is generally frowned upon by corporates (they see it as too lightweight) it can be a remarkably effective way of winning over new customers. Particularly in an environment of virtual reality, it is difficult for readers to gauge the 'feel' of a company through the standard, serious tone of the average corporate newsletter. Add your own wit and humour and more people will feel that they are making contact with a real human being rather than the electronic arm of another corporation. Offers, discounts and starter prices can also be included in your newsletter to encourage existing clients to renew orders with you, or pass your information on to potential new customers.

You can achieve some sort of layout by preparing the newsletter using desktop publishing or high end word processing software, complete with fonts, pictures and borders. However, this will be much more accessible over a modem if you compress the file using a product like PKZIP to zip it into a much smaller and more manageable format. Newsletters that are zipped can be distributed more widely and more easily to a wider audience—if that is what you want. Some forums on CompuServe take relevant newsletters for their libraries, which can then be downloaded by anyone who is interested. Alternatively, you can send the newsletter direct to a mailing list composed of your clients' Internet addresses. Take appropriate action if a respondent asks you not to send any more newsletters! An unzipped file can be large and unwieldy, and if it is not something a recipient wishes to receive you could end up the target of a hostile mail campaign. Your electronic newsletter is also, of course, an important element of your information toolset, which could come in handy if you decide to expand onto the Web.

8 Money, Tax and Legal Issues

If your efforts with the home computer look as if they might end up being profitable, or even sustainable, you may want to consider formalising the arrangement. Setting yourself up as a business sounds like a big step—and in some ways it is, especially if you didn't start out with any such notion—but in many ways it is a logical progression and a sensible, convenient thing to do. The main reasons why anyone forms a company are to:

- minimise the tax they have to pay;
- limit their liability in case of financial disaster;
- make cashflow and VAT reclaiming cheaper and more efficient;
- clarify ownership of copyright and simplify administrative procedures;
- gain additional credibility with clients.

Self-employment can be appealing simply for the glory of it, but turning your back bedroom hobby into serious work has many financial and legal implications. Like all things in life, self-employment is a series of trade-offs. Against the freedom and control you will enjoy, set the drastic diminution of your rights: quite apart from having no regular salary, you will lose holiday entitlement, sick pay provision, maternity rights, protection from unfair dismissal, and perhaps participation in an occupational pension scheme. The employer also pays a considerable share of the employee's National Insurance contributions which, as a company, you will have to shoulder yourself.

That said, there can be a bright side. The tax treatment in

Britain of the self-employed is very different from the Pay As You Earn system, and in some instances is more generous. However, even if you consider yourself self-employed, it is open to the Inland Revenue to assert that you are in reality an employee, and for them to attempt to recover (normally from your alleged 'employer') any Pay As You Earn contributions they claim should have been paid. Self-employed individuals are responsible for paying their own National Insurance contributions—but you will not be entitled to the full range of NI contribution-linked benefits.

One further implication of becoming self-employed is that you should consider carefully what insurance you will need. Expensive office equipment and furniture often justifies a separate policy, and it may be worthwhile to consider an income protection policy in the case of prolonged illness. You will also be responsible for your own pension.

FORMING THE COMPANY

If you are committed to the idea of self-employment, choosing a form of legal entity or structure for your business should be your first step. There are three types of business which are relevant to the home-worker, each of which has its own advantages and disadvantages. Each will have a major impact on the way income tax rules and regulations affect your business, which in turn will determine your legal rights and responsibilities.

A *sole proprietorship* is the least expensive to form and usually requires nothing more than a 'DBA' (doing businesss as) name and possibly a local business licence. It is a flexible, quick arrangement which confers flexible pros and cons. On the one hand, you gain maximum control over the operations of the business, but on the other, you are landed with maximum liability. It is up to you to make all final decisions and assume responsibility for all aspects of your business, and you, personally, are the one the debt collectors will come to for all monies owed. Personal control means personal liability, and although it is a risk, it is one which is often worth taking if you are going into business for the first

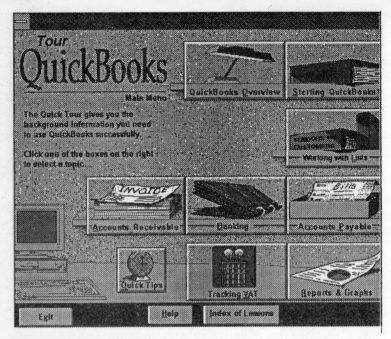

Setting up a small business often gets stuck at the first hurdle—managing the money. Whilst there is nothing to beat a real accountant, there is a lot of software available to get you through the basics of company set-up and financial management. Quickbooks, shown here, is specially designed to help non-accountants through the money maze.

time at a relatively modest level.

A *partnership* can be an appropriate business arrangement where two or more individuals want to go into business together, and can be set up as either a general or a limited partnership. Within a limited partnership, the limited partners' liability can be restricted to their financial investment in the business, the trade-off being a loss of control over key business decisions. By contrast, a general partnership—like the sole proprietorship—allows for maximum control over the day-to-day operations of your business. It is common practice to draw up a partnership agreement, where the rights, responsibilities and obligations of each partner are specified. Unfortunately, personal liability remains one of its disadvantages.

A *private limited company* has a legal identity distinct from that of the participants—strictly 'shareholders'—and liability for debt is limited. Bear in mind that a self-employed company director would almost certainly have to stand as personal guarantor for his company, thus 'limited liability' can still end up meaning personal bankruptcy. There are various tax and insurance disadvantages to incorporation, but some private individuals working through an agency as contractors prefer to set up as a company to avoid being taxed as an employee on PAYE. The trading-name of a limited company is registered and thereby given protection against rivals appropriating your name and reputation.

FINANCIAL MATTERS

Get an accountant

It need not be complicated and *can* be handled by yourself, but there are many good reasons for finding yourself a reliable accountant who can run this aspect of the business on your behalf, particularly when you are starting up. There are standardised ledgers for small-traders, but for anything more complex than simple maintenance of income-and-expenditure records (together with the appropriate invoices and receipts), it may be best to hand over all other work to a competent accountant. Accountants have a far better grasp of the procedures that need to be gone through, know where to get hold of the requisite paperwork and specialise in monitoring and optimising money flows. Nor do they have to worry about other aspects of the business as you do. Final accounts detailing profit and loss, depreciating write-offs and expenses (loan-interest, percentages of home heat and light bills, and so on) can be managed by a specialist, whose fees are usually recouped by the money they save for you.

Bank accounts

A private or domestic account may be adequate for occasional part-time work, but it is obviously sensible from every point of view to open a separate bank account—ideally in the name of the business—to handle financial transactions. It separates private and business resources (essential if you are to maintain any kind of domestic harmony), greatly eases the process of managing your business accounts and can sometimes work out cheaper—short-term free banking or other inducements may make life easier in the first year, but beware of what happens after that. Charges vary but can increase, and more so than for personal accounts, so shop around. Enquire about overdraft facilities while you're there—these are often made available subject to an acceptable business plan and can be accompanied by higher than normal interest rates. Loans are often important to enable a small business to get going, and many banks are prepared to provide loans where the interest is deductible against business taxes.

Accounting and business records

For obvious reasons it is necessary to keep books of account that are decipherable to an outsider. Limited companies must file annual audited accounts although the requirements have been simplified here, as with low-turnover self-employed operations. Accounts number-crunching may be computerised but security and data backup is essential. Other records to corroborate the books of account include receipts, bank-statements, cheque-book stubs, vehicle-mileage records, or petty-cash books. Business records generally would include an activity logbook citing proposal or contract dates, follow-up, fee analysis, project files, time-sheets and campaigns. Documented proof is more use than memory or hearsay—write it up.

Your salary

Clearly an important consideration. It is reasonable, legitimate and necessary to abstract a personal income from your business, although you may find 'drawings' (the technical term for 'salary') described as almost an optional and arbitrary consideration. Award yourself what you think is fair and reasonable—you are in charge, after all—and try to strike a reasonable balance between ridiculous modesty and outrageous extravagance. For tax purposes the sole-trader or partnership will be assessed on the net profit made by the business *after* deduction of all expenses, investment, etc. The private limited company pays its directors a salary, deducts tax from them on a PAYE basis and has employer obligations for insurance contributions and so on.

Tax

Income tax
Personal income tax is paid by the self-employed under schedule-D arrangements, direct to the Inland Revenue. It is initially levied in arrears—sometimes considerably so (useful short-term assistance) depending on trading start date. Subsequently it is paid in January and July and includes a graduated additional payment to DHSS National Insurance. Limited companies deduct tax from directors' salaries on a PAYE basis together with DHSS contributions, and are liable for employers' DHSS contributions and Corporation Tax.

VAT: Value Added Tax
Should the turnover of the business exceed a certain annual value—estimated from a quarterly appraisal and usually around the £30,000 mark—then it is legally necessary to register for, and to collect, VAT. The threshold value and arrangements for seasonal variation and altered payment schedules vary periodically and the Customs and Excise department will advise. Even if initially the business turnover is below the threshold, it may be useful to register since VAT on business expenditure and capital costs can be reclaimed. Some motor-vehicle costs may be included in return for a 'scale-payment' representative of the personal benefit to a sole-trader or partnership. Furthermore,

registration can enhance the credibility of the business, although obviously there is an increased burden in remitting quarterly accounts. This can be facilitated if Accounts computer-software includes the feature automatically.

Insurance

Domestic insurance policies specifically exclude any business usage—in extreme cases, using your back bedroom as an office could invalidate an entire insurance claim. Preempt disaster by contacting your existing insurer and advising them of your plans; many will then be happy to add an extension to your existing policy at a relatively modest premium, to cover computing equipment. It is quite a different matter if you expect to be dealing with people on your premises, however. Whether they be employees (full- or part-time) or clients, you are leaping into a separate league of insurance and will need a separate policy entirely. The same may be true if you accumulate large amounts of expensive equipment—photocopier, engineering design and printing equipment; or large file servers. For yourself, you must continue to pay National Insurance, the additional tax levied by government. Normally this is paid as flat-rate self-employed contributions through the year by bank direct-debit or by stamping a card. Depending on business profits, a further sum is payable via the income tax assessment.

Professional Liability Insurance (PLI) is something few people think of until it is actually requested by a client. It will help smooth negotiations if you have it, makes you look more professional and is generally a good idea. Depending on the work you expect to do, it may be worth your while to make arrangements for PLI only as and when it is required; alternatively, some clients may be prepared to add the risk temporarily to a corporate insurance. If your work is likely to involve any physical risks to you or anyone else, you should add Personal Liability Insurance to your policy, for which you can expect to pay more. From your own point of view, health and temporary incapacity insurance is a sensible safeguard since you will only be getting paid for the work you do. If you are starting out with capital, however, perhaps saved from a salaried job, you may prefer to rely on that to get you through low periods. Insurance is deductible as an expense, but in the early days of operation not all the desirable purchase-items can be afforded.

Pensions

Pension contributions or investments are a deductible expense and can represent a preferred investment option—the early operation of the business may allow minimal funds for even sensible investment. The age of many consultants is such that they can top up existing pension arrangements when funds permit. Whilst age does not debar you from self-employment, younger professionals may not have the advantage of existing pensions and insurances and may want to make private arrangements to take care of these matters.

PART-TIME ENTREPRENEURS

The power and sophistication of home-based computing technology have given rise to a large number of entrepreneurs who have chosen to begin their home businesses while still putting in the hours for a full-time salaried position. Clearly this is a desirable and sensible approach from many points of view (although it is hard work!), and although tax and legal arrangements do not actually discourage this type of activity, they do not particularly encourage it either. Basically, a home-based business will be treated entirely on its own merits, and no special treatment, either good or bad, will be justified because of other employment elsewhere. VAT, income tax and insurance are equally applicable to the part-timer and the full-timer. The real issues here are those which may arise between yourself as a small business and your employer, especially if you are carrying out similar work privately and also as another company's employee. If you are likely to end up taking business which might otherwise have gone to your employer, you are obviously on thin ice; more so if you use company time or resources (computing equipment, for example) to pursue this business.

LEGAL MATTERS

Unless you are confident in your own knowledge of account-ing, an accountant will be indispensable—an investment rather than an expense. Legal beagles are similarly useful, and whilst your accountant can probably advise you on the law connected with tax and finance, there are other areas where specialist expertise may prove useful now and again. It is unlikely that you will need to retain the services of a lawyer full-time, but it is probably worth befriending a solicitor who is experienced in small business law and can provide you with assistance whenever you need it. Legal advice is most appropriate when you are drawing up the paperwork you will be using—such as forms for invoices, contracts or other agreements—to ensure that you are asking for and displaying the required information. Solicitors are also valuable for checking the small print when you are asked to sign contracts by clients—the last thing you want is to find you have signed away all rights to your life's work when you initialled a contract with a client. Legal advice can illuminate the details of copyright and ownership of work, especially important where you are producing written material—either journalistic articles or software code—and it can also be indispensable if you find yourself involved in the sensitive area of libel.

Contracts

The contract is an agreement to undertake certain work for a prescribed fee with attendant conditions on delivery, pay-ment, quality, disclosure and so on. A verbal contract is legally binding, although proof of terms, other than hear-say, may be difficult in the event of disagreement. For this reason, anything of any real value or importance—including ownership of work—should be laid out in a written contract, and although it may be expedient to agree a short-term or urgent job verbally, a covering letter identifying work-content, fees, people involved, timing, delivery and payment is always a safe measure. Initiate it yourself if your client does not. If responsibility for contracts is generally going to be yours (and even if it is not), have an initial model contract drawn up by a solicitor. In the event of a commission with critical consequences in terms of money, health and safety or practitioner liability, get the lawyer to oversee the terms. Consequential loss assurance and implied conditions are 'unfriendly' areas, as are any rolling arrangements for further work without fee-renegotiation. Intellectual property rights are also an area to be wary of. Waiver of any contract conditions should be agreed in writing by both parties.

Invoicing

Invoices should be prominently identified as such and should include date, term, VAT number, name (and proprietor or registration) of the billing firm, plus the details of the payment required. Invoicing of customers for payment is often according to whatever appears in the contract small print. The tradition is to bill monthly, creating a sort of variable credit facility to customers, although that will not always be suitable. Adverse cash-flow destroys small businesses, as does overdraft interest, and there is no reason why you, as a new business, should not arrange invoicing to suit your own needs. Thus, on-completion, 15-day invoicing, part-payment in advance, and certainly 'payment at milestones' are legitimate practices to be investigated.

There's no easy way to deal with late payment, and no guarantee of prompt payment according to contract. It is an area in which most small businesses are vulnerable and, especially at the beginning of your home-based career, you are unlikely to be in a position to put any pressure on clients who withhold payment. You will find that the problem evens out over time—clients come to trust and respect you more, and are therefore more willing to 'keep you sweet' by paying promptly; and as your client base expands the through-put of cash becomes more steady. Bear in mind that large companies with many contractors are unlikely to value you sufficiently to pay you out of turn with others or to humour unusual payment terms, and are likely to have established a payment rhythm which gives them the most favourable rates. The more clients you have and the greater the diversity in their size and needs, the steadier will be your payment. Persistent late payers may respond favourably to a letter from a solicitor, but work out in advance how much you value the work and whether or not you can afford to lose it. Clients who simply do not pay are in breach of the contract and liable to legal action—again, work out the costs and benefits in advance. It may cost you less to write off a debt, learn a lesson and start again than to pursue a claim through the courts.

Libel

Defamation is a serious accusation to have against you, and one from which many plaintiffs have reaped rich rewards. So it is as well for home office enthusiasts who are writing for a living to be aware of the law of libel: defined as 'defamation published in permanent form'. Libel covers all writing, printing, drawing and photography, as well as television and radio broadcasts; slander is essentially spoken defamation and therefore of less relevance in this instance. Publication of a libel can result in a civil action for damages, an injunction to prevent repetition and even (unusually) a criminal prosecution. The plaintiff (the person libelled) must demonstrate to a court that:

- The matter complained of has been published, i.e. communicated to persons other than the plaintiff;
- The matter complained of refers to him- or herself;
- The matter complained of is defamatory, normally judged by asking:
    Does it lower the plaintiff in the estimation of society?
    Does it bring him or her into ridicule, contempt or dislike?
    Is he or she likely to be shunned or cut off from society as a result of this matter?

Those accused of libel have five defences which can release them from liability. These are:

- *Justification*: that the offending comment is true in substance and fact—here it is up to the defendant to prove it, rather than the plaintiff to disprove it;
- *Fair comment*: that the libel was in fact an honest observation made in good faith and without malice in a matter of public interest;
- *Privilege*: the 'libellous' comment was made, in the public interest, of fair, honest and accurate reports of public judicial proceedings, Parliamentary reports or other public meeting;
- *Section 4 of the defamation act*: that publication of the libel was unintentional, not intended to refer to the plaintiff or not perceived by the author to be defamatory. If this defence is accepted, the defendant must make 'an offer of amends', effectively a published apology.
- *Apology*: that no malice was intended by publication, and that an apology was published immediately or very soon afterwards—but prior to the action being brought.

Copyright law

Copyright law aims to protect the *form* in which an idea or invention is expressed rather than the idea itself; thus plots, systems, schemes and themes are not protected. Copyright confers upon the owner the right to deal with the work in a number of ways (especially selling the right to use it) and also to prevent others exploiting it. For work to justify copyright protection, it must be 'original', which in legal terms means it need only have been the product of skill and labour on the part of the author; it does not require innovative or cultural merit. Under the broad heading of 'Literary Works' which justify copyright protection, for example, come books, articles and computer programs.

Ownership of copyright *automatically* goes to the author, but an important exception is work produced by an employee in the course of his employment, in which case copyright belongs to the employer unless otherwise stated. There is thus a grey area for part-time entrepreneurs, who may be required to show that their work was produced for reasons other than normal employment, if copyright becomes disputed. This is another reason for placing some legal structure around a home-based business, in order to clarify who owns what. Where work is commissioned (and paid for), it can be argued that copyright belongs to the commissioner rather than the creator (although the automatic reversion of copyright to the creator remains in effect). Normally this would only be upheld if the creator had signed a written *assignment*—that is, a document specifically handing over copyright to the commissioner. Normal practice is for the creator to *license* the copyright, allowing the commissioner to exploit the work whilst himself retaining overall ownership. This can be done verbally.

9 Co-operation and Group Work

No one works alone. Even if you are a one-person business, you have suppliers, clients and customers, and others on whom you rely for advice and general information. For most of us, working involves some degree of collaboration with others, either within the same organisation or closely linked with it. This may be because of their physical proximity—perhaps you share an office, for instance—or perhaps between you, you produce a saleable product, even though you are separate businesses.

For example, you may be a graphic designer and your collaborator a phototypesetter who turns your artwork into film. Although you are both freelance—or separate business units, as the Inland Revenue would see it—one cannot survive without the other. And you may not work in the same location—in fact the chances are that you do not.

Or perhaps you are part of a two- or three-person business. Let us suppose that you are providing local services such as typing and computer access, so that local people and organisations can use or learn to use computers. As well as access to the computers themselves, you add personal help and advice to the equation. That is because an ability to use the computer will not necessarily mean that those using it would not benefit from guidance in tasks such as laying out a leaflet or newsletter, organising and printing out a mailing list, or drawing up a business plan using a spreadsheet.

Or maybe you are a telecommuter, someone whose job allows you to work at least part of the time from home, using modern technology to ensure that those vital contacts are maintained.

Whatever the exact nature of your organisation, you need co-ordination, to ensure that when something needs doing there is someone present whose skills meet the demand. When making plans for future projects, you need to ensure that everyone is fully involved in the decision-making process, but if you are at all busy, then you will not necessarily have the time, at the right time, to ensure that you are all in the same place to have those vital discussions. And if you are working for a larger organisation out of your home, then you could do with tuning up your communications to ensure that they work for you in the most efficient way possible.

If any of these situations, or something like them, resembles yours, then you could probably do with some help from the computers on which you either have spent, or are about to spend, a fair amount of money.

HOW COMPUTERS CAN HELP

Using a computer to stay in touch is little different in concept from conversing on the phone. But the big difference is that, unlike the telephone, computerised communications allow you to conduct business without having to be on the same timescale; in other words, to be on the phone, both parties have to be using the phone at the same time. When communicating using computers, it does not matter what the other party or parties are doing at the moment you compose your message. And, unlike the phone, you can send messages to any number of people at the same time. Of course it is true that, using the phone, you can always set up a conference call with more than one person, but the phone still loses the advantage of being able to use a flexible timescale. In practice, what computers deliver is an ability to communicate more flexibly and in ways that were impossible before, and to save you a lot of travelling time and money, too. To achieve this relies on a network.

Networks—what they are and what they offer

A network is, quite simply, the linking together of two or more computers. The rest is implementation: in other words, just how networking happens is of concern mainly to the technically minded, or to the managers of corporate networks. Do you need a network? It depends of course how many people make up your business, but with just two, probably not. With three or more, you could probably construct a good case for buying a cheap network card for each computer—you can pick one up for less than £100—and using the software built into Windows to link the machines together. The advantages you gain are, broadly, threefold.

1   *Group access to data.* Firstly and most obviously, you can get access to each other's files, while keeping parts of the PC's hard disk private to yourself. While you may not mind co-workers looking at the business letters, you will not want them peering at your correspondence with your bank manager. This can be useful if someone is out of the office and you need urgent access to a file on her hard disk. Assuming the machine is on, and that what you want is in a public area of her hard disk, a network solves the problem.

2   *Resource sharing.* You can also start sharing additional hardware such as printers and modems. That saves you having to buy a printer for each computer, or interrupting someone else's work so that you can print. Instead, you ask the computer to use the printer attached to someone else's PC, and print to it directly. In the normal course of events, the other PC user will hardly be aware that you are accessing his or her printer. That principle can also be extended to modems—the devices you use to communicate across the phone lines. If you want to link up to the Internet or to an online service such as CompuServe to pick up your mail, just tell the software to use the modem attached to the other user's machine. Alternatively, if yours is the PC with hardware attached, you can set up Windows so that it will allow others to have access to

your printer and modem, as well as your files.

3   *Email and other communications.* Some of the benefits of
    networking will depend on the extent to which you share
    data. If you are in a small business, with just a handful of
    co-workers each of whom does a different and largely
    unrelated job, there may be less justification for net-
    working. On the other hand, if you are a busy team and
    are not always in the same place at the same time, there
    is a prima facie case for setting up an electronic mail
    system, and an electronic discussion group. These will
    allow you all to go where you need to in order to fulfil
    the demands of the business at the times you need to be
    there, while remaining in constant touch with the office.

There are times, too, when everyone needs to work on the
same information more or less simultaneously, or when you
need to pass a file from one to the other, ensuring that each
person who adds to it has clearly finished with it. An example
would be a proposal for new business that you may be
generating, where each person adds something that relates to
his or her specialisation. Without a network, you could very
quickly end up with half-a-dozen different versions of the
file on different floppies, each of which had a different date
and differing contents. You would then need to go through
each version, pulling out the new bits and pasting them into
the consolidated version. That is a recipe for disaster, as
there will almost always be one person's work on the file
which, by accident, does not make it into the final version.

There's no doubt, though, that the overall benefits of
networking—sharing information and communication—by
far outweigh the drawbacks, and all predictions suggest that,
by the end of the century, most personal computers will be
networked in some way.

The potential of computerised group working

Electronic communication can take many forms. Simple
electronic mail is the closest and most obvious analogue of
the phone. But it can also be a note to all of those due to

attend a meeting reminding them when and where the meeting is due to take place. This note can often be generated by the software that not only books a room (if appropriate) but enters the booking into a central database and schedule that are accessible to all who are connected together. If one or more of the individuals cannot make the meeting because they have other appointments scheduled, the software will be able to handle that and will warn the person setting up the booking of the clash. In other words, you can eliminate all that ringing round three or more people to find a common time-slot, so long as they all use the group scheduling software to manage their calendars.

If you are working from home, the electronic mail system can keep you in touch with what is going on in the office, and ensures that you have got the latest figures and sales prices, for example. If you need to keep up to date with an ongoing discussion, you can participate using a discussion database, in which the various threads of the discussion can be clearly seen and retrieved. Threads work like this: one person makes a suggestion to which others reply. This in turn spawns a number of other suggestions, each of whose merits and demerits can then be debated in full, using separate threads of electronic conversation.

It is rather like holding a large meeting to talk about an idea, and then asking people to split up into separate groups or workshops and come back with polished conclusions for presentation to the full meeting. The difference is that because the threads are electronic and are permanently on view, anyone can join in any part of any discussion. So you do not have to decide which workshop to join: you can take part in all of them. If you need to be more structured about it, you can moderate the debate—that is, keep an eye on what is in each thread and move the discussion on when it starts to veer off-topic, or begins to repeat itself. These, unfortunately, are common hazards of electronic debates.

Electronic communications are of course especially useful if you are physically separated—you could be miles, maybe hundreds or thousands of miles, away. But imagine you are one of a group of locally based people who between you are developing a large document—it might be a technical manual of some kind; it might be a research project; or it might be a proposal for more business. You need to be sure that you are all working in the same direction, that you do not duplicate work, and that individuals do not overwrite changes made by others. Without software assistance, you can do it but you will be working in a fairly serial fashion. That is, one of you would add a piece, followed by another adding her section, and so on. Plug the computer into the equation, and you can all work on the same document, no matter where you are, as well as ensuring that those pieces which need to be finished before others get done first.

'Groupware'—team software

How does teamworking software work? The first element in the equation is relatively simple. You need a network along which to transport this information. This can consist of any kind of information transmission conduit. If you are far away from those with whom you need to share information, then the most likely conduit is the phone. If you are in the same office, then use your local area network (LAN). On top of this, you need to run some specialised, application software.

'Groupware' is the generic term in techie-speak for computer software that sits on a network and organises people, but rather than list in abstract what that is, it will make it clearer if we explain what two such products do and how they do it. We shall be looking at Sareen Software's OfficeTalk, and IBM's Lotus Notes. Both aim to add an extra dimension to the way people work together, but one is suited to small offices and groups, the other to larger concerns. The former is more suitable for an organisation involving a relatively small number of people, but we shall look at the latter as well, so that you can gain a flavour of what an industrial-strength piece of software, with all the bells and whistles, can do. That way you can decide which of the currently available products on the market deliver enough of those features to fit your needs. The point is that both are addressing similar problems.

Note that the pace of progress in the computer software industry (new products come out as often as every four to six months) means that you should not blindly rush out and buy either of these two products, as they are likely to have been superseded. Instead, look for the kinds of features that you need, or think you will need, over the next year or so.

OfficeTalk

OfficeTalk's focus is on groups of people who are involved in projects that are often different from each other, but which all need those involved to interact. So this compact—and cheap—piece of software handles project meetings, contacts and notes in separate areas of the software, while remaining easy to use. It comes on a single disk and offers a diary, task management, electronic mail and general data management. It will also handle contact management, which means, for instance, that you will quickly be able to see what was last said to the organisation's biggest creditor or customer, even if you were not the one who said it. You will also be able to save time by keeping a central registry of contact details—phone numbers, addresses and so on—because when one person alters a detail as the contact moves or changes phone number, everyone will instantly know about it.

You can easily see what facilities are on offer by the software because they are presented in simple, clear icons on buttons at the top of the screen. There is electronic mail, which can be one-to-one and one-to-many and can include attachments—files which you want to send to someone along with an electronic mail message explaining why you are sending them—as well as 'while you were out' messages. Diaries can be seen by day, week or month, and you can tell at a glance what days are full—not just your own, but everyone else's too. When you set up a meeting, the software sends an attendance request, which invitees are at liberty to turn down, on a form that pops up with the meeting request. Making all this happen is easy, as you only need to choose names from a pop-up list for events such as meetings.

The product also includes a planner view, which acts like a

wall planner and enables you to see where holidays fall, while the project planner gives you the power to allocate assignments, to set start and completion dates for the over-all tasks and sub-tasks of which it is composed. So, for instance, if you are building a large technical manual, you will need to organise it in phases, which may look something like this: research, followed by a meeting to discuss the organisation of the information you have garnered, then writing up, proof-reading, design and layout, and printing. If several people are involved, letting the software work out the deadlines and help you set priorities is likely to make your organisation more efficient. You can also get OfficeTalk to organise a routing for a document so that it goes to people in the right order and does not move on to the next in line until the recipient has done whatever it is he or she is supposed to do.

OfficeTalk is efficient, costs very little and is easy to use. Although basic compared to many more complex products aimed at large companies, it is one of the best of its kind. On the other hand Lotus Notes, which is sold by IBM, is designed for use by worldwide enterprises yet can still be used by smaller companies.

Lotus Notes

This is a big product that generally needs its own PC to run the central database which contains your information, although you can also run it on a standard Windows PC so long as only a few of you are using it. You will need someone who knows what he is doing to set it up and keep it running efficiently, yet it is so flexible that the uses you can find for it are almost endless.

It works round the concept of a shared database, which in effect means information that can be shared by all users. In practice, you do not want everyone to have free access to all the information held by a company—salary details, for example, are not good candidates for public viewing—so you can set it up so that people see only the databases that are relevant to them. Other databases you might want most people merely to read rather than add to or edit. As with

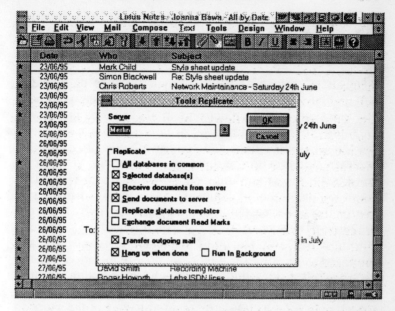

Lotus Notes, one of the most popular of the categories of software known as groupware. Its ability to 'replicate' files from a remote server to the desktop means that users can easily maintain the same files in the office at home.

OfficeTalk, you can conduct threaded discussions, but these are not limited to single locations since Notes allows you to dial into it from wherever you might be. So if you run the company on it, as many large concerns do, you have access at any time to information, discussions and documents.

If you have more than one site, you really start to use the power of Notes by allowing the databases at the different sites to replicate. This means that they swap information between them so that it is always synchronised—there is no need to worry about having the latest version of something, such as a technical drawing, because Notes makes sure it is always available. Using a feature of Notes called Notes/FX, you can even get other programs to hook into a Notes central database so that your familiar word processor could be the viewer through which you look at your list of contacts or current discussions. Notes has a high capacity, and can deal with almost any volume of information you care to throw at it.

The disadvantage of Notes is that, because of its flexibility, when you first take it out of the box it seems to have little use apart from its electronic mail. The idea is that you can build your own database structures, your own forms with which to view them, and your own Notes programs that do clever things with the data. In other words, you can do pretty much the same things with Notes as with OfficeTalk and a lot more, but it demands more work from you to achieve this. The reasoning behind this strategy is that your company will have its own way of doing things, such as arriving at and implementing the results of decisions, and that a standard solution would fit no organisation exactly since everyone does things differently, depending on their business situation. That exact fit is what Notes aims to provide—so long as you are prepared to put in the work to make it happen.

These two products have been covered only in outline, mainly because they will have been upgraded at least once by the time you read this, such is the pace of the industry. They represent the two extremes of the category of software that helps you make decisions and run the organisation, and your needs will probably fall somewhere between them.

You can contact IBM for Lotus Notes on 01784 455445, and Sareen Software on 0181 423 9434.

HOME-WORKING AND TELECOTTAGING

Much of the hardware and software we have discussed throughout the book will be useful if you are working from home. On the software front, that mainly means communications products, which provide a vital link to the many bulletin boards and online services such as CompuServe. These deliver a huge raft of information, and information is the bedrock upon which any successful freelance or home business career must rest. So check out Chapters 4 and 7, where we have gone into detail about the kinds of hardware and software you will need, and what online services are available.

If you are staying in employment and are plugged into a remote head office, then your system manager will have provided you with the tools and procedures to get linked into the company network down the phone line. You should also insist on being linked into the office electronic mail system as, without it, you will be isolated from the daily ebb and flow of office life. After all, while there are advantages to working from home, there is no reason why you should not stay in touch with those people with whom you still need to interact on a professional and personal level.

If you are thinking about setting up a business in collaboration with other local businesses—you might be serving a local community by delivering information technology (IT) services, for instance—you should think about the kinds of resources you need to share and which you will do better to bring in-house. For example, you might want to share a receptionist but not your IT technical support. An organisation set up to help in just such situations is the Telecottage Association. Specialising in rural areas, it aims to spread the use of IT in small businesses using shared facilities, and is supported by BT, Apple Computer and the Gulbenkian Foundation. It holds seminars from telecottages round the country linked up by video phones, and publishes a magazine called *Teleworker* which is sold on the newsstands. More than eighty telecottages now exist.

Whatever the structure of the small office, you will clearly need a form of networking system, the precise details of which will depend very much on the amount and type of information you need to share. For many small businesses, the networking system included in Windows will suffice, for a while anyway. This works by allowing everyone to share all or part of the information that is stored on their hard disk. However, the limitation of this approach is that it depends on each individual obeying certain rules to ensure that information does not get lost or overwritten and that it is always available. Often it is simpler in the long run to set up a central network computer (known as a file server) into which everyone can link. The file server is never switched off, and you can concentrate your resources on making sure this machine stays switched on and working. You will need cabling, hubs (small devices that act like telephone exchanges, to which all the PCs are connected) and a network interface card for each PC to slot into one of its expansion slots. A piece of software known as a network operating system to run on your file server—most people use either Novell NetWare or Microsoft Windows NT Server—completes the picture.

A complete rundown of the pros and cons of the various components that go into building even a small network could fill this book, so we suggest that you find a basic book about networking, and then approach a local reputable computer dealer for more practical help.

Once you have set up the network infrastructure, you will find that most modern application software products (such as Microsoft's Word or Novell's WordPerfect) allow you to share the information they process quite simply and transparently.

The kinds of decision support product (groupware) that we have outlined above will aid your ability to share your thoughts and expertise with others, and vice versa; none of these products is specific to telecottaging because different situations will call for different emphases on the various features of the product you pick. So you might, for instance, find the project planner highly useful but the discussion database feature less so because you have other means of making decisions. For up-to-date information on the latest products you will find the specialist trade press useful, particularly those magazines that compare several similar, competing products in a single review.

Computerisation can help your organisation by giving you more time and greater flexibility, and by improving internal communications. Decision support software allows you both to keep in touch with co-workers and to run the organisation without always having to be in the same place at the same time as everyone else. This frees you to go and hunt for new business, to talk to existing clients, or even to take more time off.

Working with others is so often a matter of co-ordination—making sure that everyone is pulling in the same direction, which often means checking that everyone knows what the others are doing. Computers are good at this sort of thing. So long as they are given the information to start with, their automation skills can make your organisation more efficient, more responsive, and more fun to run. Go for it.

Reference Material

Bass, Steve. Top picks for the home office, *PC World*, Dec 1994, v12, n12, p281(2).

Bibby, Andrew. Taking the decision: is telework right for you? extracted chapter, with minor updating (1994), from *Home is Where the Office is: A Guide to Teleworking from Home*, Hodder & Stoughton, London 1991. © Copyright 1991, 1994 (CompuServe Library File).

Bock, Wally. *The View from Cyberspace* (Copyright 1994), CompuServe Library File.

Bournellis, Cynthia. SOHO what?, *PC Week*, July 18 1994, v11, n28, pA14(1).

Bray, Paul. Cottage industry, *Which Computer?*, July 1993, v16, n7, p46(5).

Brown, Donna. Working at home: too much of a good thing?, *Executive Female*, Jan–Feb 1994, v17, n1, p76(1).

Bukowitz, Wendi, Landaiche, Mickey. The crossroads of commitment (goal-setting in small businesses), *Home Office Computing*, July 1991, v9, n7, p38(2).

Buskin, John. Isolation paranoia (the psychological dangers of working at home), *Home Office Computing*, Jan 1994, v12, n1, p84(2).

Call, Barbara. Women in computing should work to integrate, not isolate themselves, *PC Week*, April 21 1987, v4, p43(1).

Christensen, Kathleen. Remote control: how to make telecommuting pay off for your company, *PC-Computing*, Feb 1990, v3, n2, p90(5).

Davidson, Jeffrey. Supporting your life's priorities, *Supervisory Management*, Nov 1992, v37, n11, p6(2).

Dvorak, John C. Domestic bliss, *PC-Computing*, Dec 1994, v7, n12, p75(1).

Dvorak, John C. SOHO? Ho ho! *PC Magazine*, Jan 25 1994, v13, n2, p93(1).

Edwards, Paul, Edwards, Sarah. Just say no to distractions, *Home Office Computing*, Oct 1990, v8, n10, p40(1).

The Gordon Report. British telework expert offers telework contingency plan, *Telecommuting Review*, May 1993, v10, n5, p1(3).

The Gordon Report. British conference on 'teleworking' highlights trends, *Telecommuting Review*, Nov 1 1988, v5, n11, p14(1).

The Gordon Report. Commentary: shining up the crystal ball once again, *Telecommuting Review*, Jan 1993, v10, n1, p1(8).

The Gordon Report. Doctoral dissertation probes personality differences between home and office workers, *Telecommuting Review*, Dec 1 1988, v5, n12, p6(4).

The Gordon Report. Face-to-face meetings: when and how to use them, *Telecommuting Review*, Jan 1 1988, v5, n1, p8(3).

The Gordon Report. Telecommuting and child care: a case study in short-sighted management, *Telecommuting Review*, May 1 1992, v9, n5, p1(2).

The Gordon Report. The older (home)worker: a talented labour pool waiting to be hired by the pragmatic employer, *Telecommuting Review*, May 1 1988, v5, n5, p10(4).

The Gordon Report. Time, love and tenderness: commentary on changes in birth rates, use of time and feelings about work, *Telecommuting Review*, Feb 1 1992, v9, n2, p10(3).

The Gordon Report. Work-from-home experts describe psychological profile of 'open collar' workers, *Telecommuting Review*, Oct 1 1988, v5, n10, p7(3).

Haughton, Emma. Top marks for home work, *Computer Weekly*, June 25 1992, p40(2).

Kane, Karen. Women are heading home, *Home Office Computing*, Oct 1990, v8, n10, p10(1).

Karon, Paul. Telecommuting: home work for professionals

(can mean greater productivity, but not for everyone), *EDN*, Oct 18 1990, v35, n21A, p105(2).

Lewis, Peter H. A tight fit, *PC-Computing*, July 1989, v2, n7, p159(2).

Mancey, Joanna. Working nomads, *IBM System User*, Dec 1993, v14, n12, p52(3).

Mathiesen, Mike. *Marketing on the Internet* (CompuServe sample file).

McGee, Mark. Sensational SOHO software, *Computer Dealer News*, Nov 15 1993, v9, n23, pS17(2).

McGinn, Janice. Thinking about teleworking? Get it right, and it can pay big dividends, *Computergram International*, Oct 20 1992, pCGI10200008.

Milano, Carol. Conquering isolation, *Home Office Computing*, April 1991, v9, n4, p21(3).

Mitchell, Horace (*Management Technology Associates*). Telework: Perceptions and Reality. Extracts from a report based on the experiences and attitudes of UK managers and teleworkers.

Mulkern, Tom. *Online Marketing Strategy*, Issue 1.1, February 1995. Electronic newsletter © 1995 (MLC) CompuServe Library File.

Orrange, Kate. Telecommuters gain ground; computer firms creating guidelines based on trial runs, *InfoWorld*, Feb 14 1994, v16, n7, p10(1).

Poor, Alfred. Going SOHO, *Computer Shopper*, Dec 1994, v14, n12, p182(7).

Schafer, Liza. More women are becoming their own bosses, *Home Office Computing*, Feb 1991, v9, n2, p10(1).

Schepp, Brad. The best opportunities for telecommuters, *Home Office Computing*, Oct 1990, v8, n10, p49(3).

Smith, Leslie. Home alone, the sequel, *Executive Female*, May–June 1992, v15, n3, p56(1).

Solberg, Ron. *Using Bulletin Boards, Internet, and Online Services to Promote Products and Services*, CompuServe Library File 1995.

Speeth, Lauren. Critical factors for telecommuting success: do you have what it takes to succeed as a telemanager? *Telecommuting Review*, Sept 1 1992, v9, n9, p4(2).

Strangelove, Michael. Advertising on the Internet: Frequently asked Questions and Answers, *Strangelove Internet Enterprises*, Inc Version 1.0, March 6 1994.

Sullivan, Nick. Burning the home-office oil, *Home Office Computing*, Dec 1990, v8, n12, p100(1).

Sullivan, Nick. It's 1993: do you know where you're going?, *Home Office Computing*, Jan 1993, v11, n1, p112(1).

Sullivan, Nick. Minding business, minding kids, *Home Office Computing*, Jan 1990, v8, n1, p112(1).

Wallace, Peggy. Are you ready to support telecommuters? *InfoWorld*, Sept 5 1994, v16, n36, p57(2).

Wooten, William, Burroughs, Wayne A. Setting measurable goals for better performance, *Supervisory Management*, Dec 1991, v36, n12, p3(1).

Zeidenberg, Jerry. The SOHO phenomenon, *Computer Dealer News*, Nov 15 1993, v9, n23, pS3(1).

Magazine for home office workers

Home Run, published ten times a year by Active Information, Cribau Mill, Llanvair Discoed, Chepstow, NP6 6RD. For subscription information, telephone 01291 641 222 or fax 01291 641 777.

Home Run continues practical information for anyone who wants to go it alone, whether as a teleworker, consultant or freelancer; for someone making or selling products, marketing a service or acting as an entrepreneur. It also provides a forum for the exchange of ideas, information and encouragement to help mitigate the sense of isolation many may feel when they are no longer part of a large corporation.

Index